Fit to Die

Men and Eating Disorders

Anna Paterson

Lucky Duck is more than a publishing house and training agency. George Robinson and Barbara Maines founded the company in the 1980s when they worked together as a head and psychologist developing innovative strategies to support challenging students.

They have an international reputation for their work on bullying, self-esteem, emotional literacy and many other subjects of interest to the world of education.

George and Barbara have set up a regular news-spot on the website. Twice yearly these items will be printed as a newsletter. If you would like to go on the mailing list to receive this then please contact us:

e-mail newsletter@luckyduck.co.uk   website www.luckyduck.co.uk

ISBN: 1 904 315 40 2

Published by Lucky Duck Publishing Ltd.

Commissioning Editor: Barbara Maines
Editorial team: Wendy Ogden, Sarah Lynch. Mel Maines
Designer: Helen Weller

Printed in the UK by Antony Rowe Ltd.

Biography

Fit To Die is Anna Paterson's fourth book, Her first book Anorexic (Westworld International, 2000) was an autobiographical account of her 14 year struggle with anorexia. Her second book Diet Of Despair (Lucky Duck, 2001) was a self-help book for eating disorder sufferers and those who care for them. Her third book Running On Empty (Lucky Duck, 2002) was a novel for young people about eating disorders and friendship. Running On Empty won a Times Educational Supplement NASEN Award in 2002 and Diet Of Despair was also commended by the judging panel.

Anna is now recovered and spends her time trying to help other eating disorder sufferers, who contact her daily. She works to raise awareness about the reality of these illnesses and is regularly asked to speak about her experiences. She lives with her fiancé Simon, who helps her with all aspects of her work including editing her books.

This book is dedicated to Raphael Teff – a very kind and
thoughtful man, who is sadly missed.

I would also like to thank Simon for his dedication
to this project and his constant support.

In addition, I want to thank The Author's Foundation
& the K. Blundell Trust.

Contents

Introduction

I myself suffered from anorexia nervosa for 14 years and when I was asked to write a book specifically on men and eating disorders, I was curious to discover whether there were many differences between the experiences of male and female sufferers. Up to this point, my contact with men suffering from the illnesses had been relatively limited. When I was in Heath House Priory Hospital, a fellow patient was a young man suffering from bulimia. Like many people, I hadn't realised that men suffered as deeply with disordered eating as women and was very surprised to hear that he had many similar feelings to myself.

Gradually, as I began writing books on eating disorders, I found that a greater number of men started to contact me. Their problems initially seemed quite different to those suffered by the women who wrote to me. However, when I talked with them I realised that the root causes and the overwhelming feelings they suffered with were very similar. This is why *Fit To Die* has been designed to complement my previous self-help book on the subject, *Diet of Despair*.

At the root of all eating disorders is low **self-esteem** and this is as much an issue for men as for women. However, men have the added problem that our society says they should be 'strong' and so showing their emotions can be very difficult.

In this book, I have tried to explain many of the problems that men encounter and give positive ideas to start overcoming them. Throughout the book, I have emphasised that eating disorders are serious conditions. If you have picked up this book because you feel you may be suffering from one, I would strongly advise that you seek medical help as soon as possible.

Part One

Learning About Men & Eating Disorders

Chapter 1

The Hidden Disorders

Eating disorders are usually considered to be 'female' illnesses and although a large percentage of sufferers are women, there is now a growing number of men who are also suffering. It is still unclear exactly how many eating disorder sufferers are male, as research into men and eating disorders is twenty years behind that of women. However, estimated figures range from 10% up to 33%.

As society is gradually beginning to accept eating disorders as a serious problem for women, it is still not recognising that men are also struggling with body image issues. Unfortunately, it has been reported that some doctors still do not recognise cases of either male anorexia or bulimia. Men are also often afraid to speak openly about their food and weight problems, in case they are seen either as 'feminine' or 'gay'.

Originally it was assumed that the majority of male sufferers were homosexual. However, over time it has become increasingly clear that although a number of male eating disorder sufferers are gay, a high percentage are heterosexual. A recent study identified only approximately 20% of male eating disorders sufferers as gay. It has also been noted that many young men developed their eating problems before they became sexually mature and realised they were homosexual.

When men do find the courage to visit their doctor, they may be told that they are suffering from other conditions or even that they do not have a problem at all. A young bulimic male suffering with enlarged lymph nodes due to constant **vomiting** was initialling diagnosed as possibly suffering from cancer. His doctor did not even consider that his low weight and enlarged glands could be due to anorexia or bulimia.

Men may also find it hard to recognise that they have a problem themselves. Whereas women are constantly kept informed by the media about cases of anorexia and bulimia, men rarely see evidence of the condition. Unfortunately, this means they are less likely to seek help early on in the development of their condition. On average, it seems to be approximately six years before men will seek help for their eating problems and by this time the condition will have become chronic. Often, their eating problems are only identified when they visit the doctor with a related issue, such as joint or muscle problems from excessive exercising.

Even when men do choose to seek help for their condition, the services available to them are usually not extensive. Many health providers have not considered providing specific services for men. This often means that if men choose to have treatment, they are sometimes the only male in female only support groups or hospital wards.

It has been noted that whenever there is a specific media campaign aimed at raising awareness of the problems of male eating sufferers, the number of people asking for help increases dramatically. When men have been questioned about their eating disorders, it has become clear that they would like to know more about the subject. They would like to be able to talk openly with other male sufferers and have access to male treatment programmes. Due to feelings of shame about their condition, it seems that men are currently more willing to use helplines than join in with support groups.

Often the length of time that men wait before asking for help can mean that they are in support groups or hospitals with much younger sufferers, who are usually female. This can leave them even more isolated and less able to open up and share their feelings. Being in a group with even just one other man enabled them to identify problems that were gender specific and which related solely to their masculinity and self-image. For example, men and women experience **puberty** differently and the way their body changes can play a vital role in their levels of self-esteem. Women are often concerned about developing into a curvaceous woman and want to lose weight in order to keep their body child-like. Men are more likely to be concerned if their body does not develop fully and will feel inferior if they do not have a defined musculature. They also need to discuss different issues to women, since they hold a different role in society.

Eating disorders in men is still an area that is very under-researched. Although treatment for both men and women seems to be quite similar, there are many different problems that affect men only. For example, women are always asked if they have ceased **menstruating** (have their periods stopped?) as this is a classic symptom of anorexia nervosa. However, men are not asked if they are still having early morning erections, which would similarly indicate a change in their hormonal levels in the body.

Like women, men suffer from all the various kinds of eating disorders although binge eating seems to be the most prevalent problem. There are also differing concerns for both men and women. Research has shown that women are more concerned with their weight, whereas men tend to focus on their shape and muscle definition.

There does not seem to be a specific age at which men develop eating disorders and sufferers have been known to range from as young as eight to men in their sixties. However, the majority of men with eating disorders state that their problems began during their childhood years. Many remember being overweight in their teens and as a result were singled out and bullied or called names. It does seem that whereas women are more likely to be at a normal weight when they develop an eating disorder, men are frequently overweight.

The original reasons why they were overweight as children are frequently linked to problems at home, crises at school or difficulty coming to terms with growing up. This low self-esteem coupled with the issues surrounding their weight can lead to eating disorders. As the numbers of overweight children is increasing, it is very important that teachers and parents are aware of the effect that being overweight can have on a child and the possibility of eating disorders developing.

Like women, men are also at risk of different types of **abuse** during their childhood years (mental, physical and sexual). Research has shown that many male eating disorder sufferers experienced childhood sexual abuse. This is often an experience which men feel unable to discuss due to feelings of shame. They are concerned that they will be accused of 'bringing the abuse upon themselves'. Often, victims blame themselves and feel certain that others will blame them too.

It is now widely acknowledged that eating disorders are a way of coping with the stresses of life. Traditionally, men are known to turn to drink or possibly drugs as a way of dealing with the issues in their life which they find impossible to solve. In contrast, women are seen as more frequently turning to eating disorders for their 'solution'. It now seems that these boundaries are beginning to blur however and as society changes and places more importance on men 'looking good', eating disorders are increasing in the male population.

Stresses frequently increase at specific points in a person's life and this can trigger a dormant eating disorder to become active. For example, a number of men have stated that when they went to college, their eating disorder became worse. Other stressful times can be during a relationship break-up, illness of a parent, starting or changing a job and starting or changing a school or college.

It has been reported that men often change their diet or exercise habits when they see a parent fall ill, especially if the illness is diet or weight related. Fear of having similar health problems such as heart disease or a stroke can cause a man to radically change his dietary habits and this has been shown as a cause of some eating disorders developing.

Men are traditionally more emotionally withdrawn than women and this means they often find it very difficult to discuss their feelings. Sufferers have specifically stated that they found it impossible to talk with their peers about their eating problems. They commented that the 'macho' culture meant that they were afraid their friends would think them 'weak' or 'feminine' and that they would lose all their respect. This is another reason why it is of vital importance to men that they can access good treatment services and talk with sympathetic professionals.

It is ironic that men often do not admit to problems with food, as they feel they will be thought effeminate and yet as their illness develops, they naturally lose their masculinity. Muscles begin to waste away, **testosterone** levels drop and they lose the defined masculine shape.

With the development of feminism, many women have felt free to objectify men's bodies in the way that theirs have been treated for so many years. This has meant that men have started to feel self-conscious about their body shape. They are constantly seeing images in magazines, on billboards and on television of the 'perfect' male body. It seems that in the same way that women are expected to have the 'perfect' size 8 body, men are expected to have 99.9% lean muscle definition. Men now have their own body beautiful magazines and *Men's Health* has become a top seller. Like women, men have now started to count **calories**, exercise daily and constantly compare themselves to the models on the magazine covers.

It seems that it is men in their teens, 20s and 30s who are most affected by the imagery that is now portrayed by adverts and other media agencies. Older men grew up in a time when the male body was hidden. For example, in movies and television shows, men did not bare their body.

It also seems that the 'ideal' male shape has changed. A recent study has compared the action figures of the 1970s and 1980s with those of today and there has been an enormous increase in the musculature. In 1974, a GI Joe doll (the American equivalent of Action Man) had a 44 inch chest, 31 inch waist and 12 inch biceps. The GI Joe of today has a 50 inch chest, 28 inch waist and 22 inch biceps. It seems that an increase in musculature, especially on the upper body, is the new 'desirable' shape. Recent male role models have been extremely muscular. Film stars such as Arnold Schwarzenegger, Sylvester Stallone, Dolph Lundgren, Vin Diesel and all the WWE wrestling stars portray the image that large muscles and power are essential masculine traits.

This increasing trend for such muscular bodies is a concern. Some researchers do not believe that it is possible to have a figure of the proportions demonstrated by the dolls without resorting to the use of steroid supplements. Certainly there has been an increase in the number of men resorting to supplements to try and increase their size and muscular definition. Anabolic steroids are very dangerous medications and can cause psychotic reactions such as hallucinations, manic symptoms and depression.

Studies have begun to show that bodybuilders share many of the same problems as eating disordered patients. Some have developed muscle dysmorphia or 'reverse anorexia' as it is now often called. This is a condition in which the sufferer feels they can never be large enough. Although they can actually be very muscular, they are convinced that they are small and fragile. Sufferers may increase their protein intake by 20 to 30 times that which is normal and this is very dangerous.

It is becoming more obvious that men feel a need to have a muscular body and equate thinness with weakness and frailty. A study of US college males found that when men were asked to pick their ideal body type, they chose a picture showing a man with approximately 28 **pounds** more muscle than they had on their own bodies.

Of course there are large numbers of men who do not have traditionally muscular bodies and who do not feel a strong desire to bodybuild. These men can often be left feeling inadequate and with a strong hatred for their own body. It can cause them to strive for a different shape – a lean, toned body. However, this is when problems can develop. Coupled with an already low self-esteem, these young men can take their dieting or exercise routine to an extreme and an eating disorder can result.

Often body image obsessions go unnoticed if the young man appears healthy and is engaging in what we see as healthy behaviours - exercising and watching his diet. While working out regularly is healthy, excessive exercise can be extremely damaging, especially if it is done to try and calm body image fears.

Men are far more likely to turn to exercise to deal with their body shape issues than women, who usually choose dieting. When a study was carried out on American college students, it found that 63% of the women were on a diet as opposed to only 16% of the men. However, a large percentage of the men were concerned about being too small and 28% were trying to gain weight, often by bodybuilding methods. The evidence suggests that exercise related illnesses such as muscle dysmorphia are far more common amongst men than women.

As our culture changes and men are marketed in a similar way to women, other problems have developed. Men are now expected to be well groomed, well toned and conscious of their health and diet, as well as strong and robust. This is causing a dilemma. There is the quest to be lean and trim, which is in contrast with the need to be strong and muscular.

The fashion industry responded to the need for men to assert their masculinity and the 'sportsman' look emerged. Designer sports clothing and trainers are hugely popular amongst the young male population and present an image of toughness and masculinity.

Men are spending more money on their fitness and this is a growing trend. A survey has found that men today are spending 58% more on fitness related activities than in the five years previously. A large percentage of the economy is now dependant on the current fixation with thinness for both men and women. It has been reported that men's dissatisfaction with their body has tripled over the last thirty years. In increasing numbers, men are having plastic surgery and **liposuction** has become especially popular. Between 1999 and 2000 there was a 23% increase in the number of cosmetic procedures performed on men.

Eating disorders in men (as in women) are not about food or weight but are in fact emotional problems. They develop as a way of coping with the conflicts, stresses and pressures in life. An eating disorder may seem like a way of exerting control for a person who feels that their life is out of control.

Theorists have proposed that there is a link between body image and personality. The body has become a 'screen' onto which the person projects their feelings. For example in the case of anorexia sufferers, by becoming thin to the point of emaciation, they are subconsciously trying to show how deeply they are suffering emotionally.

The onset of a eating disorder in males is usually due to a specific trigger or triggers. Surveys have established some of the specific triggers for men. These include:

- Experiences of childhood bullying and/or teasing due to being overweight.

- Developing psychological problems such as low self-esteem because of issues during childhood (examples of which are incest, rape or mental torment).

- Problems at home such as parental strictness, especially from a father. This often extends to control over food and ritualised mealtimes.

- Bodybuilding and obsessive exercising. This may be linked to the cultural and social pressures young men are under to develop a 'perfect' body.

- Specific occupations such as athletics, dance, horse racing, etc.

- A previous history of being overweight. This may be linked to a **genetic** problem, such as **obesity**, which can run in families.

- Difficulties dealing with their own homosexuality.

- Having a parent who is suffering from a serious weight related illness such as heart disease or **diabetes**.

- College students who are away from home for the first time may feel under intense pressure to fit in and can suffer extreme emotional stress that develops into an eating disorder.

- A fear of developing sexual feelings. Anorexia causes a drop in male testosterone levels, which leads to a lack of sexual feelings and desires.

- A desire to remain in a dependant relationship with their mother due to a fear of the traditional masculine role they should adopt as an adult.

- For older sufferers triggers may include: excessive job responsibilities, divorce, marital problems, children leaving for college and the death of a parent or close family member.

As mentioned above, it appears that men are more at risk of developing an eating disorder if they participate in certain jobs or sports that have weight restrictions, such as wrestling, bodybuilding, swimming, horse racing and gymnastics. It has been discovered that 8% of male athletes in Norway suffer from some kind of eating disorder. Another survey found that when they questioned athletes in the sports of boxing, weight-lifting, karate, wrestling and judo they found that 82% had used unhealthy methods such as **laxatives**, **diuretics** or diet pills to try and control their weight.

Runners are also at an increased risk of developing eating related problems. The National Runners' Survey on Dieting and Eating found that 21% of the men who answered the questionnaire were terrified of gaining weight. In other studies, it was discovered that they also seemed to have a preoccupation with food similar to that of an anorexia sufferer. They would strive to constantly lower their percentage of body fat, even when this was already very low. Many had lost 25% of their original weight and showed a relentless pursuit of thinness as well as often having a disturbed body image.

A condition known as 'Anorexia athletica' has recently been diagnosed and is specific to athletes. It is characterised by several features similar to Anorexia nervosa but without the self-starvation practises. Their severe weight loss is instead brought about by prolonged and excessive exercising.

Jockeys are also known to use many different methods of weight control prior to a race. Food **restriction**, excessive sauna usage, laxative and diuretic abuse, appetite suppressants, excessive exercise and self-induced vomiting can cause them to lose up to 7 lbs. in fourteen hours. All of these practices are extremely dangerous and very detrimental to their health. Some other professions that may cause participants to be vulnerable to eating disorders are modelling, dancing and being a flight attendant since these all necessitate weight limitations.

There do seem to be some specific differences between the way that men and women view themselves. Women specifically seem to worry about whether they are fat or ugly but with men it is usually slightly different. They are more concerned with how they see themselves, and their self-worth is linked to how strong, in control and productive they are in their lives. They need to feel a success in all areas of their life – work, exercise, background, friends, home life etc. If a man feels inadequate in different areas of his life then it is possible that problems can develop.

It is said that women "dress to impress" but men in contrast work out to compete with other men. There is a strong competitive element in most men that leaves them feeling inadequate around any man who has a tighter, more muscular body. Men who have smaller bodies are often considered 'weedy' and used in advertising campaigns as figures of fun – for example the Mr Muscle cleaning products campaign. This can lead men to feel that unless they have a strong muscular body, they are a failure.

Many opinions and ideas are formed by watching television and it is very obvious that this medium does not portray society accurately. Americans are seen as slim and fit and rarely shown as overweight or obese. When a survey was carried out, it revealed that only 6% of men and 2% of women on television were obese. These figures show that society still finds it slightly more acceptable for men to be overweight than women. Obese men were seen as strong and characters such as Cracker, Ironside and Perry Mason confirmed this fact. Large women were seen as much less acceptable and were usually either stereotyped as black or lower class, such as Roseanne.

As women's achievements and competence in the home and workplace has changed, so has the balance between male and female roles. When men feel threatened, they can resort to trying to change their shape to impress and assert more power in relationships. This change in shape allows them to redefine their entire identity.

Films such as Fight Club have highlighted the confusion that men feel over their role and identity in society and how they try to deal with unexpressed emotions such as aggression or competitiveness. This confusion over gender roles can lead to eating disorders developing in both sexes during adolescence.

It has been established that there are certain personality traits linked to eating disorders. Males suffering with these illnesses tend to have dependent and **passive-aggressive** personalities with a tendency to avoid conflict. A dependent personality needs constant approval as well as affection and will often feel the need to please others. They are afraid of conflict and try to avoid stating their needs or desires for fear of displeasing others. They try not to behave in an assertive manner in case this is interpreted as aggression. They are very insecure and feel afraid of being abandoned, which leads them to ask for constant reassurances that they are loved.

Often eating disorder sufferers are unable to provide internal comfort for themselves and therefore behave in a manner that will ensure they receive a continual supply of comfort from external sources. This is frequently what leads them to become people-pleasers. Unfortunately though, this type of behaviour can often have a negative effect as loved ones will tire of constantly trying to give reassurance.

Passive-aggressive behaviour is common amongst eating disorder sufferers. It can develop when a child is given mixed messages. An example of this is when a child is told that they are loved but the parent is speaking in an angry voice. This can eventually leave them confused and with deep-rooted feelings of ambivalence towards both themselves and others.

Children respond constantly to their parents' reactions. When a child begins to show independence, it is the parents' reaction that can determine whether or not the child is able to accept themselves. If a child is led to believe that it is wrong for them to be venturing out alone then they can develop feelings of helplessness, inadequacy and shame. If the parents are too overprotective or put too many barriers in a child's way then this can lead to an eating disorder developing in later years. The child grows up feeling dependent on the parents and does not feel able to leave home at the appropriate time. An eating disorder allows them to remain a 'child' who is protected and looked after by the parent.

A stifling family atmosphere may also prevent a child from developing their own personality and behaviour patterns. They may turn to anorexia as a way of achieving a separate identity and asserting some control over their life even if this is in a negative manner.

When a child starts school they come into contact with other children both of their own age and older. They are then plunged into a competitive atmosphere in which they have to assert their own personality. Often popularity is based on appearance and negative comments about their body size or shape can lead to inferiority complexes developing. Isolation often follows and as they grow up, boys can be scared of venturing out in case they receive further taunts. If they do receive any further humiliation, this can confirm their worst fears and they become more withdrawn. This can then lead to an eating disorder developing as they try to change their body shape.

Men who develop eating disorders frequently do not tend to conform to the traditional masculine ideals. They seem to veer more towards the more traditional female personality traits – passivity, a lack of physically aggressive behaviour, neatness, dependency on others and a desire to please. This can lead to them being bullied throughout their childhood and an eating disorder can result as they begin to feel disgust with their own body.

As with women, men do not always fall neatly into one particular defined eating disorder since they may suffer from a variety of symptoms from all the conditions.

These unspecified eating disorders are usually classed as **ED-NOS** (Eating Disorders Not Otherwise Specified) and can be just as dangerous physically and psychologically as the other listed eating disorders. All eating and exercise problems are likely to require professional help.

Certain atypical eating disorders have been identified, such as a fear of choking, which leads to restrictive eating and symptoms similar to those of Anorexia nervosa. Another documented condition is emetophobia - a fear of vomiting, which again causes the sufferer to exhibit anorexic-like symptoms.

Throughout this book, I will explain each eating disorder in more depth and discuss ways of helping sufferers to accept, understand and eventually beat their illness. If you have picked up this book because you are concerned that someone you know has an eating disorder, these are some of the first signs to watch for

◉ An obsessive preoccupation with their diet, body, weight and shape.

◉ Eating a limited or restricted diet.

◉ Over-exercising and/or using products to increase muscle size.

◉ A noticeable change in body size and shape.

◉ Vomiting after meals (often indicated by disappearing to the bathroom immediately after eating) or abuse of laxatives and diuretics.

Chapter 2

A History Of Men and Eating Disorders

Throughout the ages, disordered eating amongst men has been evident. During the height of the Roman Empire for example, wealthy men ate until their stomachs bulged and then visited a vomitarium to make room for the next course. Today, their behaviour would definitely be described as bulimic.

The first case studies of anorexia in males were reported between 1689 and 1790. In 1689, Richard Morton described the very first case of male anorexia as 'nervous consumption'. He was presented with a 16 year old man who had lost his appetite for no physical reason. The loss of appetite coincided with working too hard at his studies. When the young man abandoned the work, he then began to recover.

The ideal male body image has also varied through the ages. In Ancient Greece, a young, perfectly formed athletic physique was the 'ideal'. At that time, physical perfection was linked with intellectual and spiritual attainment.

In the 19th century, the philosopher Nietzsche promoted the idea of the 'Ubermensch' or 'Superman'. The Nazis in Germany in the 1930s later adopted this, in a twisted form. They promoted the idea of a heroic, muscular, emotionless, strong male role model to which all German men should aspire.

Ancel Keys demonstrated the link between dieting and a flawed relationship with food in the 1940s. A controlled experiment was set up using 36 male conscientious objectors. As the experiment progressed and the subjects received a limited diet, their relationship with food and with their own body shape began to change. Cravings for high fat, high sugar foods became apparent and the men developed a continual preoccupation with thoughts of food.

This study put forward the idea that dieting could lead to the development of cravings, which could then trigger binges. Depriving the body of the required nutrients caused the mind to focus almost solely on the need for nutrition. The fact that many more women that men dieted was one of the reasons why it was felt men were less likely to develop eating disorders than women. More recently however, men have begun to develop similar attitudes towards food and weight as women and this could be linked to the rise in eating disorder cases amongst the male population.

Throughout history, many famous figures have exhibited weight and body image problems. The poet Byron was described as 'gloriously handsome except for a double chin' which it was reported troubled him greatly. He would resort to a diet of only boiled potatoes and water until he felt that he had lost sufficient weight.

In England, the royalty have not been exempt from weight problems. Henry VIII was renowned for his vast size in later years and a special suit of armour had to made for him. King Edward VIII (who was later to abdicate the throne to marry Wallace Simpson) was reported to have suffered from anorexia during his childhood years. It is believed that the strictness of his father and a harsh Nanny caused him to develop the condition.

The name Charles Atlas is one that most people have heard and associate with bodybuilding. In 1903, Charles Atlas moved to the United States from his home in Italy. In addition to being an immigrant, he was not physically gifted and was often beaten up by bullies. After spending an inspirational day at the zoo watching the strong and powerful lions, he decided to start to develop his body. By the age of 17, he had pioneered a technique that is still used by men today to achieve physical fitness.

His technique was called 'Dynamic Tension' and it transformed him from a 97-pound youth into the man who won the 'Most Perfectly Developed Man' contest at Madison Square Gardens in 1922. He continued to enter contests and also began modelling. By 1928, he was constantly asked so many questions about his physique that he joined up with Charles Roman. Together, they developed the 'kicking sand in our faces' campaign and within months were both millionaires.

In the 1950s, the American Medical Association even endorsed the Atlas course in 'Dynamic Tension' and baseball stars such as Joe Dimaggio were among the pupils. Charles Atlas was heralded as an all-American hero who could save 'weak and feeble youths' and turn them into powerful men.

Gradually, more celebrities have felt able to talk about their eating problems. An American magazine recently printed an article on the actor Billy Bob Thornton, who spoke openly about his brush with anorexia nervosa. Other famous people who suffer with eating problems have included the singer Luther Vandross, who has repeatedly gained and lost weight throughout his career. Prior to suffering from a stroke, his mother had spoken about his eating, which she said was completely out of control.

Elvis Presley is another star renowned for his problems with food. In 1958, during his induction into the army, publicity photographs showed Elvis as lithe, supple and taut. He was portrayed as the perfect patriotic American citizen.

However, in time, binge eating led him to gain large amounts of weight. It wasn't just the quantity of food that he was eating which caused the problems. Elvis frequently consumed very high fat foods. His favourite meal was reportedly peanut butter and banana sandwiches grilled in butter. Another famous meal he enjoyed was 'Fool's Gold Loaf'. This was a hollowed out white loaf, drenched in butter and then stuffed with peanut butter, jam and bacon. Coupled with a heavy prescription drug problem, this harmful behaviour caused Elvis to die at the age of only 42.

Currently there are two body types that dominate the pages of the male magazines. The first is the slender, sculptured look of actors such as Hugh Grant, Toby Maguire and Jim Carrey and the second is the muscular, pumped-up shape of bodybuilders such as Arnold Schwarzeneggar. Both of these iconic images are very different from the heroes of the 1940s to 1970s. In those eras, the leading men included Kirk Douglas, John Wayne, Burt Lancaster, Steve McQueen and Burt Reynolds. They seemed to have almost an indifference to their appearance and this made them even more appealing to women.

In the 1980s, a change occurred and it became the decade of jogging, healthy eating and **aerobic exercising**. Hollywood stars produced their own exercise videos and advertising campaigns began to feature male bodies. A particular advertisement campaign by Calvin Klein set a new trend. Their models were hairless and lean, with an almost feminine look.

As men started to feel a need to change their bodies, attendances at gyms increased, as did the sales of Men's Health and other associated magazines. The first male supermodel was Marcus Schenkenberg and when he released his autobiography, he revealed that to keep in shape he did 650 abdominal crunches each day. Liposuction is also increasing at a greater rate for men than women. Figures state that it has increased by 30% for men, as opposed to only 20% for women.

Men are also traditionally portrayed as strong and emotionless. The Clint Eastwood 'Man With No Name' character in the mid-1960s personified the strong, silent, loner male role model. President Richard Nixon in the 1970s prided himself on being emotionless and showed no sign of tears during his impeachment. Coupled with the rise of the all-action hero (for example Rambo and the Terminator) this all served to leave men feeling weak and 'feminine' if they showed any feelings.

There definitely is an inequality between the sexes, especially in the media. Women are often assumed to be anorexic when they are overly thin, whereas men such as Mick Jagger or David Bowie (known as 'The Thin White Duke') do not receive the same press coverage.

In 1990, Robert Bly wrote a book called 'Iron John'. He had noticed that a new breed of men had started to develop who were unhappy with the idea of hurting anyone. They had grown up during the Vietnam War and wanted nothing to do with a manhood that required them to fight an enemy. They were no longer single-minded and instead were receptive to different ideas and viewpoints. These so called 'soft males' were kind and gentle human beings but they were often unhappy because of their passivity. Bly tried to show that it was possible to be both sensitive and powerful. This began a new men's movement and drum-beating, back to nature seminars were established to enable men to go back to the source of their masculinity.

In addition, the film industry has begun to address the problems that larger men are experiencing and the film *The Full Monty* tried to deal with issues of male self-image. This was a film about six redundant steelworkers who put on a strip show and by 2002 the film had pulled in over $80 million dollars. One of the six men is considerably overweight and throughout the film struggles with low self-esteem. At one point he states, "You'd better pray that women are more understanding about us. Anti-wrinkle cream there is. Fat bastard cream there isn't."

The media are also more likely to portray women as obsessed with their weight but men as obsessed with their level of fitness. Men's magazines focus strongly on weightlifting, bodybuilding and muscle training, whereas women's magazines are usually more concerned with diets. This is the predominant image of our society – boys are taught to be proud of themselves if they are strong and athletic, girls are taught to value beauty.

Chapter 3

Anorexia Nervosa In Men

Anorexia nervosa is a life-threatening condition. The sufferer refuses to maintain their weight at a healthy level and over time becomes emaciated. They feel terrified of gaining weight or becoming 'fat' and develop a distorted view of their own body size and shape.

Anorexia is often caused by body image disturbance. This is when a man has distressing thoughts, fears or worries about his body. This then leads to preoccupations about how they can change their body by altering their diet, increasing the amount they exercise or even by radical surgical procedures.

In the majority of cases, anorexia nervosa begins with the sufferer voluntarily dieting. As time passes though, the dieting gains momentum which causes the sufferer to lose control. He becomes unwilling and feels unable to return to a normal diet and healthy weight. It seems to be the level of self-control and willpower that determines whether a sufferer develops anorexia or bulimia. If a sufferer cannot restrict their intake for long enough to lose dramatic amounts of weight then they are more likely to start the binge/vomit circle and develop bulimia.

As mentioned previously, eating disorders begin for a large number of different reasons. Anorexia nervosa can also serve a number of different 'functions' for the sufferer.

- For boys and teenagers, it can be the 'solution' to a developing crisis either at home or at school. The eating disorder soon takes up all their time and other problems are pushed aside.

- For adult males, it can be used to 'deal' with problems in their relationship, marriage or at the workplace.

- For all ages, the sufferer feels that they gain a sense of control over their lives with the anorexia. The may feel powerless either at home or school and turn to the eating disorder to change that.

- The sufferer develops a 'sick' role in the family and no longer has to make decisions for themselves. They are comforted and looked after, as they had been when they were a child. They illness 'protects' them and they do not feel that they have to join the adult world with all the responsibilities that entails.

- When a child is discouraged from expressing themselves openly, they may turn to an eating disorder in order to develop an 'identity'. Gradually, over time, they 'become' the eating disorder and feel terrified of giving up their 'sick' identity. Recovery will mean developing a whole new healthy identity, which can feel very threatening.

The psychological profile of men with anorexia seems very similar to that of women suffering from the illness. Both groups suffer with depressive and obsessional thoughts. As the emaciation develops, the obsessions grow stronger and in response the **depression** becomes deeper. Men with anorexia (like women) will also develop serious physical problems. Unfortunately there can also be long-term damage from anorexia. If the sufferer is under 18, their growth is stunted and bones do not develop fully.

Studies have shown that men with eating disorders often have an even lower bone density than women suffering from the same condition. This means they are very susceptible to **osteoporosis** (or 'brittle bone disease'). It appears that men who suffer from binge/purge bulimia have the lowest bone density of all. The drop in bone density is linked to the lack of the male hormone testosterone. As a young man loses weight, his hormone level drops (as it does in women) and this causes bone density problems.

Many anorexia sufferers are also involved in high impact sports such as running and this can put huge pressures on their already weakened bones. Frequently, it is joint or bone problems that cause men to visit their doctor for the first time rather than their actual eating or body image problems.

Sperm production is also greatly diminished in men who weigh less than 25% of their ideal body weight. Male marathon runners and top athletes have also been found to have a lower level of testosterone. When a sufferer's weight drops below a certain level, tests show a decrease in the production of pituitary **gonadatropin**. It is this which leads to a reduction in the output of testosterone and causes infertility.

Levels of these hormones in the body will increase as a sufferer's weight returns to normal. However, there is sometimes a delay as the sufferer often still has abnormal eating patterns during the recovery period. If the sufferer experiences a low weight from a long period of time during a key growth stage then the testes may shrink and sperm production is reduced. It is possible that infertility may be permanent.

It is still unclear at what age men are most likely to develop eating disorders such as anorexia nervosa. Puberty is frequently a time when young girls develop food related problems. As their body develops, they lose the boyish figures of childhood and become curvaceous and it is this change that can trigger feelings of 'fatness' and self-hatred. For young men, puberty often occurs between two and three years later than it does for girls, and they do not gain body fat but actually lose fat and develop muscle instead. If a man matures early and develops well, he is likely to feel more self-assured and confident. Women who develop early often feel isolated, different and have low self-esteem. However, if a young boy does not develop at puberty then he is more likely to experience body issues. A young man who feels he has an under-developed physique may turn to bodybuilding as a way of increasing his musculature. Taken to extremes, bodybuilding and obsessive exercising can lead to serious health problems.

Chronically ill male anorexia sufferers will have gone through various stages during their years of illness. Restricting food, **bingeing** and vomiting, excessive exercising, laxative and diuretic abuse as well as taking diet pills are all common behaviours. If the sufferer has been ill for a number of years, it is possible that they switch between periods of anorexia and periods of bulimia.

Anorexia is an illness that can recur at different times during a sufferer's lifetime. If a person is going through a particularly difficult time then they may return to their old 'coping' mechanism. For example, I was contacted by a manager in his early forties who was married with a small child. His work started to become difficult as sales fell and the firm became filled with an influx of young, attractive male workers. He felt excluded as they constantly chatted about their evenings at the gym and so in an attempt to fit in, he enrolled in the club himself.

Gradually, the gym became an obsession and he spent time there every evening. If he was prevented from attending the health club at weekends, he would become difficult and moody At the same time he started to watch his diet and cut out what he considered to be 'fatty' or 'unhealthy' foods.

A pattern was emerging, which was a recurrence of an earlier problem. In his youth, he has suffered from anorexia nervosa. It had begun at school when he was picked for the sports team. In an attempt to please his parents and his coach, he threw himself into his training. As he trained, he lost weight and he saw this as improving his performance. The more miserable he felt, the more he thought that losing weight would help him to feel better about himself. The exercise and dieting allowed him to blank out the other problems that he had and this pattern then repeated itself later in his life.

It is very important to recognise the warning signs of a recurring eating disorder. Most sufferers are very aware of the fact that they may be going down a familiar path. However, often it takes pressure from a friend or family member before they are willing to look at changing their behaviour.

From recent studies, it does seem that anorexic males show a considerable amount of anxiety about sexual feelings and relationships. In fact they seem to show more anxiety than female sufferers of the condition. Frequently, males in their early twenties showed strong feelings of 'disgust' when asked about sexual relationships and seemed fearful that they would become 'trapped' or 'too closely involved' with a partner. Frequently, male anorexics have never had a sexual relationship before they developed the illness. It also became apparent that often the men came from families where the subject of sex was taboo.

Starvation and over-exercising causes a reduction in sexual drive and this allows sufferers to temporarily resolve their feelings of conflict over their sexuality. It may be that they are fearful they have homosexual tendencies and disappearing into anorexia can allow them to become asexual for a while.

Traditionally, men have a fear of becoming 'feminised' if they spend too much time in the presence of women. There is a belief that their masculinity will be 'stolen' from them if they have a close relationship with a woman. The psychoanalyst Sigmund Freud made several studies based around this idea and developed the concept of 'vagina dentata' (a vagina with teeth that could castrate men).

Many male sufferers of anorexia have been brought up by a strong feminine figure and they have lacked a masculine role model. This has led them to state that they see themselves as more feminine than masculine in their attitudes and behaviours. They had stronger feelings of sadness, guilt and were more emotionally expressive as well as being sensitive and often moody. These are traits that are more traditionally feminine than masculine. They also seem to lack the strong **assertiveness** of many males.

Difficult family relationships can be one of the root causes of the development of anorexia. When questioned, many sufferers stated that they had abnormal relationships with their parents. Overprotective mothers did not allow their sons to develop the necessary skills needed for adult life. They grew up ill equipped to handle situations as an adult male and instead turned to the 'protection' of the anorexia. Angry, distant and strict fathers can also lead to the development of an eating disorder due to a lowering of self-esteem and self-confidence.

Body image problems frequently start in childhood and continue to develop through the traumatic years of puberty. Often, the fears of obesity may be imagined rather than a reality. However, the resulting feelings for the sufferer are the same.

Anorexia sufferers usually have a different idea of what they feel is the 'perfect' body shape. Healthy adult males stated that they felt the ideal body shape was a full-chested, thin-waisted V-shape. Anorexia sufferers chose 'lean, toned and thin' as the ideal. In the past, strength and a muscular physique was vital for survival and even though today the majority of jobs for men are much less physical, healthy teenage boys still strive for a strong muscular body rather than one that is thin.

Below is a list of the diagnostic criteria of anorexia. If you suspect that you (or a loved one) are suffering from this illness, it may help to look through the list to see if you can recognise any of the symptoms. If you feel that you connect with a few of the criteria, it is strongly recommended that you seek professional medical help.

Physical characteristics of anorexia nervosa

- A low body weight, which is at least 15% below the expected healthy weight for age and height.

- Muscular weakness, a lack of energy and general fatigue.

- A lowered body temperature, blood pressure and pulse rate.

- A fine covering of baby soft hair (**lanugo**) over the whole body.

- Thinning or loss of head hair.

- Irregular heart rate.

- A lowering of the testosterone level and a lack of sexual libido.

Typical emotional and mental characteristics of anorexia nervosa

- Severe feelings of depression and hopelessness.

- Emotional withdrawal from family and friends, resulting in feelings of isolation.

- An intense fear of putting on weight or becoming fat.

- Inflexible 'all-or-nothing' thinking. This may also be referred to as 'black and white' thinking.

- Have a strong need to always feel in control.

- Have difficulty expressing their feelings to others.

- Have a perfectionist streak which leaves them feeling a failure much of the time.

- Have problems concentrating and focusing on tasks.

- Have low self-esteem and self-worth. They use their ability to lose weight as an indicator of their worth.

- Often feel irritable and snappy.

- Live in denial, believing that others are making a fuss about nothing.

- Decreased interest in sex and sometimes have intense fears about sexual relationships.

Typical behavioural characteristics of anorexia nervosa

- Extreme restrictive dieting, including fasting for long periods.

- Preoccupation with food and weight.

- Constant weight checks using scales and also measuring parts of the body.

- Unusual food rituals, such as cutting food into tiny pieces at mealtimes.

- Compulsive exercising for long periods of time.

- Deceitful behaviour – lying to family and friends about how much food has been eaten. Sufferers may also develop tricks to dispose of food.

- An inability to eat with others, which can lead to secretive binge eating.

- Disgust for their own body and strong preoccupation with certain body parts – buttocks, stomach, etc.

- A distorted view of their own body, believing that they are 'fat' when in fact they are extremely thin.

Contrasts and comparisons between male and female anorexia sufferers

The symptoms and features of anorexia nervosa do seem to be very similar for both males and females, with only a few small differences. Both groups display a strong fear of weight gain and a preoccupation with body shape. Females tend to use laxatives more than males, who usually turn more to excessive exercise as their method of weight control.

The onset of puberty is more likely to be a contributing factor for girls developing anorexia than boys. Girls can find the changes in their body shape distressing – the development of hips, thighs, breasts and stomach, etc. In contrast, boys tend to be more content with the pubertal changes. Their shoulders broaden, they grow in height and often become leaner.

Although anorexia is a hidden illness for both sexes, men are often able to keep their illness unnoticed for longer. Parents are usually very aware of the dangers of eating disorders in teenage girls but do not assume their teenage son could have similar problems. It is also quite common for teenage boys to be naturally tall and thin, particularly if they have an athletic hobby.

Relationships are a common fear for both male and female sufferers, and the disorder can develop in an attempt to avoid intimacy. Low self-esteem, shyness and inexperience seem to be common factors for all sufferers. However, in general it does seem that men express more sexual anxiety than women.

There are quite significant differences in the age of onset of the disorder. Girls often start dieting at around the age of puberty, especially if they are early developers and reach puberty before their peers. For males, the age of onset seems to be later, with the late-teens and early twenties as more common.

Men are far more likely to be medically obese before they develop their eating disorder whereas females frequently perceived themselves as 'overweight' prior to dieting, when in fact they are a normal size.

Females are more likely to desire a lower than average weight than males, who are usually more concerned with body shape and muscle definition. Many female anorexics become very competitive, especially when they are in units with other sufferers. Certain studies showed that male sufferers in contrast seemed to display a fear of competitiveness in their lives.

Both sexes exhibit a high level of perfectionism and obsessiveness. Males seemed to display more anti-social characteristics, as well as a higher level of hysterical and histrionic outbursts. Females seemed to show more maturity than their male counterparts.

Both sexes suffer from depression, anxiety and obsessions throughout the illness. However, it was male sufferers who were more likely to draw attention to any physical suffering they were experiencing.

Men and women discuss their problems differently. Women are likely to complain about how much weight they have gained in pounds and talk about how tight their clothes feel. Men, in contrast, will talk about the perceived abnormalities in their body shape and will discuss muscle groups such as abs and pecs.

Both sexes find plausible reasons for their dieting, with men often choosing health reasons. They will state that they want to avoid heart problems or diabetes in later life. Some male eating disorder sufferers say that they began dieting after watching a parent deal with weight related health problems. This is not a reason that women normally give for beginning to diet.

A lack of a menstrual period is a very easy diagnostic criteria for eating disorders in women. Unfortunately, there is not an equivalent test for men and although testosterone does decrease, this is not easily measurable.

It seems that men with anorexia are more likely to binge and vomit than women. One study found that one third of women with the disorder exhibited this behaviour, whereas 50% of the men engaged in binging and vomiting.

In previous years, it was thought that men were less likely to feel society's pressure to be a 'perfect' shape. However, this is now changing and the recent increase in male fitness and lifestyle magazines may play a crucial part in the increase in male eating disorders.

Chapter 4

Bulimia Nervosa in Men

Bulimia nervosa is characterised by a secretive cycle of binge eating followed by vomiting and/or **purging**. The sufferer will feel a compulsion to eat large quantities of food and then the resulting feelings of guilt will lead them to find ways to rid themselves of the food. The methods used are vomiting (although this is rarer in men than women), purging by taking large quantities of laxatives, excessively exercising or fasting.

Male sufferers seem to have fewer bulimic episodes than females and are less likely to turn to vomiting or laxative abuse but will instead use over-exercising as a way to rid themselves of excess calories. One male sufferer said that, "a day at the gym is a day that I don't have to throw up." Continual exercising left him feeling safe enough to eat, since he knew exactly how many calories he had burned during his work-out.

Over time, for many bulimics, vomiting can become an automatic behaviour and may occur immediately after eating without inducing it. It can happen between twenty and thirty times a day and becomes the sufferer's 'job'.

As with women, men frequently feel so ashamed of their behaviour that they will go to any lengths to cover it up. One male model suffering from bulimia felt so ashamed of his obsession with body size that he removed all the mirrors from his apartment and covered every window and reflective surface. He also felt unable to face the food deliverymen and so installed a dog flap to allow him to receive food orders anonymously. As time passed, his self-esteem dropped so low that he rarely left his apartment and found himself living like an animal, sleeping and eating on the floor. Food became his only comfort but eating led him to constantly vomit to try and maintain his model figure.

Due to their feelings of shame, male sufferers often take even longer than women to seek help and many have exhibited the illness for up to seven years before starting treatment. As with women, male bulimics are very good at hiding their illness and many function well in high powered jobs.

Bulimic males appear to be much more sexually active than male anorexics, both prior to and during their illness. Whereas a high percentage of anorexic men feel terrified of having a sexual relationship, only a very small percentage of bulimia sufferers seem to feel this way.

There also seem to be distinct character differences between sufferers of bulimia and anorexia. Those with bulimia appear to be more impulsive and less tolerant of continual discomfort and distress, as opposed to the very single-minded obsessional, perfectionist anorexics.

Typical physical symptoms of bulimia nervosa

⦿ Suffering from serious dental problems, since constant vomiting causes stomach acid to erode tooth enamel.

⦿ Exhibiting frequent weight changes due to the binge/vomit cycles.

⦿ Suffering from oedema (water retention) due to laxative abuse.

⦿ Having an electrolyte imbalance (due to vomiting) that can lead to serious heart problems.

⦿ Suffering from 'chipmunk cheeks', as the salivary glands swell due to irritation from the continuous vomiting.

⦿ Frequently suffering from constipation due to laxative abuse and fasting.

⦿ May suffer from stomach and oesophagal tears or ruptures due to the constant vomiting.

⦿ Suffering from a lack of energy, feelings of lethargy and fatigue.

Typical emotional and mental characteristics of bulimia

⦿ An intense fear of gaining weight and becoming 'fat'.

⦿ Constant self-evaluation of body shape and weight, coupled with feelings of being 'fat' and 'ugly'.

⦿ Feelings of low self-esteem, inadequacy and being a failure.

⦿ Experiencing associated feelings of depression, loneliness and self-hatred.

⦿ Having difficulty expressing their feelings.

⦿ Having a need to constantly please others.

⦿ Withdrawing from social situations and becoming isolated.

⦿ Having a strong need to be in total control of their food intake and feeling that they lose this frequently.

Typical behavioural characteristics of bulimia

- Experiencing recurrent bouts of binge eating, followed by purging to prevent weight gain. Bulimics will have at least two binges (often more) per week.

- Having a lack of control over the amount of food they eat. The sufferer is overwhelmed by a feeling that they cannot stop eating, even though they often feel physically sick from too much food.

- Excessively using laxatives, diuretics and/or diet pills on a daily basis.

- Experiencing periods of restricting food and dieting to try and control their weight, followed by bingeing when they lose control.

- Frequently begin hoarding, stealing and hiding food for private binges.

- Experiencing a need to weigh themselves and measure specific body parts, such as arms, thighs and stomach on a daily basis. Many sufferers will weigh themselves many times a day, especially before and after binges.

Bulimia is harder to diagnose than anorexia. Sufferers of anorexia exhibit emaciation whereas bulimia sufferers often remain at an average weight. Some anorexics feel that they have 'bulimic' episodes when they binge uncontrollably. However, in many cases a binge for an anorexic is just an extra salad. In contrast, a bulimic that is at a normal weight can eat up to 10,000 calories in a very short period of time.

There are specific criteria that doctors can look for when they suspect a patient is suffering from bulimia:

- Low levels of potassium – frequent vomiting and laxative abuse affect the salt balance in the body and potassium often becomes severely depleted.

- Salivary glands may also be enlarged due to irritation from stomach acid during vomiting.

- There may be damage to the stomach or oesophagus due to the constant vomiting.

- Dental problems.

- The sufferer may also exhibit other addictive illnesses, such as drug or alcohol problems.

- By talking with the patient, the doctor may also discover underlying family problems or that the sufferer has a job which requires weight restrictions.

Bulimia is a very dangerous illness. Not only are there the obvious problems brought on by constant vomiting and laxative abuse but there are also other hidden dangers. Bulimia sufferers often find that their weight yo-yos from high to low, depending on the amount they are bingeing, vomiting and fasting. These dramatic changes in weight can be very damaging to the heart.

As with all eating disorders, it is treatable and if you or someone you know is suffering from this illness, medical help is essential.

Chapter 5

Compulsive Overeating in Men

Compulsive overeating is as common for men as it is for women although often it goes untreated because men are often just considered to have a 'healthy appetite'. It is characterised by periods of uncontrolled, continuous eating which takes the sufferer past the point of feeling full. However, unlike bulimia, there is no purging after eating although the sufferer may frequently try to restrict their diet in an attempt to lose the weight they have gained.

Although with eating disorders such as anorexia the numbers of male sufferers are far lower than women, with binge eating the levels are approximately equal. It seems that men do not react as strongly as women to bouts of overeating. They do not feel such intense self-hatred and therefore are less likely to indulge in purging or vomiting. Vomiting is four to five times more prevalent amongst women with eating disorders than men.

Typical physical characteristics of overeating

- Constant weight changes, although often the sufferer will be very overweight.

- Tiredness due to the disordered eating.

- Health problems associated with obesity such as diabetes, heart problems and high blood pressure.

- Joint problems caused by carrying too much weight.

- Difficulty walking or taking physical exercise due to excess weight.

Typical emotional and mental characteristics of overeating

- Low self-esteem and feelings of self-hatred and disgust.

- Feelings of guilt and shame at their behaviour, which cause them to become even more secretive.

- Feeling disgusted about their body size.

- Using binge eating to numb their emotions, relieve tension, cope with feelings of anger, depression and other emotional problems. Often, compulsive over-eaters are said to be 'eating to fill an emotional void'.

- Trying hard to please others and feeling afraid of conflict.

- Suffering with feelings of depression, moodiness and irritability.

- Often having perfectionist tendencies and feeling that they constantly fail.

- A general sense of being out of control.

Typical behavioural characteristics of overeating

- Recurrent bouts of binge eating that continue past the point of feeling full.

- Storing, stealing or hiding food for private binges.

- Eating very fast (often without even tasting the food) for a prolonged period of time.

- The sufferer will eat even though they do not feel hungry.

- Often eating very little in company and bingeing in private.

- Eating throughout the day, with no planned mealtimes.

Particular groups of men are more likely to find themselves caught in the trap of overeating. One case study showed a young man who had always been larger than average and as a child, was often teased about his weight. At the age of eight he began to realise that he was gay. Although at that age he did not understand the full implications of this, as time passed he realised that being gay and overweight was perhaps not the best combination.

Although he had some short relationships, he felt that they always ended because of his weight. He found it hard to fit into the weight-conscious gay scene and believed he was rejected because of his size. The majority of the people he knew were constantly at the gym because they understood the importance of the 'perfect' body and this left him feeling an outsider. As a result, he ended up spending more time with his family, which left him with even less time to find a partner. He felt lonely and depressed and so turned to food as his comfort. The vicious circle was established.

Men are expected to be strong and in charge of every situation. This includes not crying when they are struggling with difficult inner feelings. Large numbers of men feel under pressure from their peers to drink large quantities of alcohol, eat fast food and have a busy social life. This can lead to developing feelings of self-hatred, shame and guilt if they do not match the expected masculine image. A long distance truck driver traditionally eats large quantities of fried food, chocolate and carbonated drinks. He is thought of as the strong silent loner but this may not be the truth. It is possible that he may hate himself because he cannot deal with all the weight he has gained.

Obesity in the UK

Sadly, in Western society, being large or overweight is not seen as 'desirable' and is still viewed as a sign of weakness and laziness. Although a high percentage of the population is now above average weight, they are frequently still laughed at or teased.

Obesity is defined as having a **Body Mass Index** higher than 30. This is usually classified as between 30 and 45 pounds over the average weight for a person's height. In simpler terms, men with a 40 inch waist or above are likely to be obese.

In the UK, it has been stated that two-thirds of men are now overweight and one in five of these men are obese. The levels of obesity have tripled in the last twenty years and the levels are still rising. These figures are worrying, since there are health problems associated with obesity. Diabetes, heart disease, certain cancers, stroke, back and joint pain, osteoarthritis, breathing difficulties, depression, infertility and sleep problems are just a few of the many health concerns.

A combination of widely available fast foods and a more sedentary lifestyle seem to have increased the problem. It is important to remember that sufferers of obesity are not necessarily eating large quantities of food each day. If a person eats just 100 calories more than their body requires every day then they will gradually put on weight and over a number of years, this can lead to obesity problems. Daily energy consumption has decreased by 20% since 1970. More hours are spent sitting watching television and using computers. Automated appliances such as washing machines, cars, dishwashers, etc. have led to a reduction in physical activity.

The UK government has recognised that obesity and weight related health problems are on the increase. In August 2002, the lorry drivers' trade association supplied their members with a new handbook, which contained healthy eating guidelines. It suggested that overweight lorry drivers should try to lose weight in sponsored events to raise money for charity. Drivers were advised to opt for healthy, nutritional food and snacks rather than choosing meals from greasy spoon cafes. It further suggested they keep a supply of fresh fruit (in particular bananas) in their cabs, together with a plentiful supply of fresh water.

Obesity is an increasing problem in the UK, not only for adults but also children. This generation is the first in 100 years to have a shorter life expectancy than their parents. Official figures show that obesity among 15-year-olds has doubled to 16% in recent years. In 2002, 16.6% of boys and 16.7% of girls (between the ages of two and fifteen) were obese.

The risk of a child becoming obese is also increased if their parents have issues with their weight. Compared with children whose parents are a healthy weight, boys aged between two and fifteen, with two obese parents, are 12 times more likely to be obese, while girls are 10 times as likely.

A number of government forums have been held to try and look at ways of dealing with the problem. It is estimated that there are now approximately three million children in the UK who suffer from obesity. A pilot scheme has been implemented in 500 schools countrywide to try and tackle this growing problem.

Vending machines and tuck shops are being stocked with healthier items such as fruit, vegetables and yoghurts rather than just chocolate bars, carbonated drinks and crisps. Other programmes are also being started, such as cookery clubs that teach healthier eating practices. There are also moves to change the content of school lunches. Another government project is aimed at infant schools, with one million children being given a free piece of fruit at their break.

It has been noted that obesity is responsible for 31,000 premature deaths per year in the UK and pressure groups are calling for a change in the advertising of food aimed at children. Many of the fast food retailers give away free toys as an enticement for younger customers. Food at burger bars are also very cheap, which is an added incentive for children. Bought individually in a corner shop or petrol station, an apple can cost anything between 25 and 75 pence. A hamburger now can cost as little as 69 pence, making it very appealing to teenagers.

Children need to be taught early about the values of healthy eating. Unfortunately, due to pressure of time, many children are brought up on a diet of convenience foods. As Professor Robert Souhami of Cancer Research UK recently stated: "If the grown-ups opt for fast food TV dinners, they can't expect the children to relish helpings of fruit and vegetables."

In the last few years, there has also been a significant increase in the size of chocolate bars and other snack foods such as crisps. The food industry has claimed that the new super-size bars of chocolate are aimed specifically at the 3% of the population who engage in high level sporting activities. They have also stated that the larger chocolate bars are meant for sharing. However, these chocolate bars are widely available to everyone in garages and newsagents, and each bar contains the calories equivalent to a full meal.

It is refined carbohydrates such as chocolate bars, crisps, cakes and biscuits that are causing many of the problems. As a small part of a balanced diet, these products are fine. However, their consumption does affect the body in significant ways and can lead to overeating. These products can have an addictive quality. When consumed, they supply an immediate boost of sugar which provides instant energy. However, this passes quickly and the consumer then craves more of the food, so that the energy boost is repeated. Unrefined carbohydrates such as cereals, wholegrain breads and potatoes release their energy slowly, keeping the consumer satisfied for longer. The blood sugar level remains constant rather than dipping dramatically, which leads to cravings.

There are significant periods in life when people are more likely to gain weight. For men this seems to be between the ages of 35 and 40 years, as well as after marriage and following retirement. These are the times when watching your dietary intake and your levels of physical activity are particularly important. Men also need to try and avoid gaining extra weight around their midriff area, as this is more likely to put a strain on their heart. Men gain weight in a different way to women and unfortunately commonly develop a 'beer belly', which can be damaging to their health.

To help shoppers improve their health and fitness levels, Tesco supermarkets decided in 2004 to introduce a new 'Trim Trolley'. This is a standard trolley with extra fitness attachments, which enable the customer to do a work-out as they shop. By setting the 'Trim Trolley' to a resistance level of 7 out of 10 (deliberately making it harder to push), the average person would burn up 280 calories during a 40 minute shop.

Obesity is also a significant problem in America and the situation is reaching epidemic levels. An American company called Sprint has designed a university campus in such a way that employees exercise more frequently during the day. Departments are set well apart so that lecturers and students have to walk longer distances to reach their next classes. They have also deliberately made the stairways very spacious and welcoming, whereas the lifts are small and slow. Many of the staff on the campus have already shown a significant weight loss since starting work there.

One in forty Americans technically qualify for stomach stapling operations due to their size and weight. However, stomach stapling operations cost up to 30,000 dollars and many insurance companies will not pay out for them. In Texas alone, obesity currently costs approximately four million dollars a year in associated medical expenses.

In South Africa, a doctor working with eating disorder sufferers has recently put forward an interesting idea. He had noticed that in South Africa, larger people had fewer health problems relating to their size than overweight people in Western countries. This raised the question as to whether the associated health problems were linked to the stress caused by the prejudices against the overweight rather than just the weight itself.

Chapter 6

Muscle Dysmorphia

Muscle dysmorphia is a syndrome seen in both men and boys who feel dissatisfied with their body. They do not believe that they are muscular enough. This will lead them to try and work even harder to build their muscles, and dangerous patterns of over-exercising begin to develop. When they look in the mirror, sufferers of this condition see someone who is small and frail, even though in reality they are usually very muscular. This condition is often known as **Reverse Anorexia** or **Bigarexia**.

Often, body dissatisfaction starts during the childhood years. Real or imagined obesity can leave a child feeling isolated and different from their peers. Early bullying or other negative feedback from family members or classmates can lead to weight related problems developing in the teenage years.

There are a number of symptoms common to people who have this condition. Like other eating disorder sufferers, a man with muscle dysmorphia frequently has very low self-esteem. Other people may admire his body but he is still left feeling inadequate. He is likely to place all his hopes and dreams into his work-outs rather than into his daily life. Often, he will even change his job because of his obsession and many sufferers try to find work in a gym or as personal trainers.

He can also become very withdrawn from others and try to avoid social situations. He is unlikely to have a girlfriend, even though many women may find him attractive. His self-image is so poor that he is convinced he is not yet muscular enough to attract women.

Exercise, diet and his appearance become a full time obsession. Sufferers will spend 90% or more of their time focusing on how to change their shape. They usually find it impossible to pass a mirror without studying their reflection. Some sufferers will check their appearance up to 50 times a day.

In the same way that anorexics will be affected by how much they weigh, people with muscle dysmorphia will be affected by what they see in the mirror. If they feel they are looking particularly small, they will pile on extra jumpers and other heavy clothes to bulk themselves up, even if it is the middle of summer.

Their mood is also usually affected by how much exercise they do each day. If they are unable to exercise, even for just a few hours, they can start to feel trapped and often become very angry. This will naturally affect their personal relationships. Partners may be unable to understand the obsessive exercising or the constant need their loved one has for reassurance about how they look.

As the illness develops, sufferers are likely to become even more inflexible, which usually leaves their partner feeling ignored and unloved. Some sufferers will not even have physical relations with their partner since they feel a need to save all their energy for gym work.

A number of sufferers do have long term partners although frequently the relationships do not survive because the sufferer does not have enough room in his life for both the illness and his partner. Ironically, often a sufferer believes his partner will leave if he is not muscular enough and yet it is the constant drive to exercise that eventually pushes them away.

Men with muscle dysmorphia are suffering in a very similar way to those with anorexia nervosa. Both groups feel shame and hatred of their own body, concern about their diet and depression. Also, like anorexics, men with muscle dysmorphia risk seriously damaging their bodies. They will continue training even when they are injured or in pain. They will also exercise while desperately hungry, allowing themselves to eat only very low fat, high protein diets.

However, anorexics compare their bodies to those of others to see if they are smaller whereas muscle dysmorphia sufferers compare themselves to other men to see if they are bigger. As time passes, body appearance becomes the only basis for their self-esteem. Any real or perceived loss of muscle tone or size causes the sufferer to feel intense shame.

Insecurities and shame about their body cause sufferers to continually hide in thick, bulky clothing. They will often refuse to undress in a doctor's office and avoid showering at the gym because they feel unable to strip in front of other men. Some sufferers feel such shame about their body that they will only work out at home. They cannot bear allowing other gym members to see their 'poor' muscle definition.

Friends and family often start to become very critical as they see the obsession growing in their loved one. They are likely to find it hard to understand why he is choosing to throw away a successful career so that he can exercise all day.

Large amounts of money are frequently spent on gym memberships, personal trainers, expensive home gym fitness equipment and dietary supplements. This can lead to serious financial problems, especially if the illness has caused the sufferer to lose or give up his job.

Eating habits become very disordered. Sufferers may try to avoid certain complete food groups such as carbohydrates or fats. Alternatively, they may begin consuming only dietary supplements in the form of protein shakes for example. This very limited and strict dieting can lead to occasional binges on carbohydrates and fat rich foods, especially when the sufferer is very hungry after a strenuous work-out.

It has been noted that there seems to be a strong link between muscle dysmorphia and compulsive overeating.

The combination of excessive exercise, disordered eating and possible steroid abuse can cause serious physical problems to develop. Muscle dysmorphia sufferers can experience exhaustion, low body temperature (which may lead to hypothermia), high blood pressure and a lowering of testosterone levels, which can result in a diminished sex drive. They may also suffer from restlessness, depression, anxiety, mood swings, a sluggish **metabolism** and be very susceptible to injury. In addition, they can suffer weight related problems - for example, over-developed legs which can chafe and bleed.

Many sufferers understand that they are damaging their bodies but feel they cannot stop their negative behaviour and they are driven on by the obsessive nature of the illness.

Reasons why muscle dysmorphia develops

As with all eating disorders, muscle dysmorphia often develops for a combination of different reasons. The illness can begin with the sufferer believing that they are just trying to become healthy and get in shape.

The following are some of the reasons why muscle dysmorphia may develop:

The sufferer experienced frequent teasing during childhood and adolescence for being 'too thin', 'weedy' or 'a wimp'.

Our society promotes the message that 'real men' are muscular. Men have been bombarded with images of muscle rippling heroes. Many sufferers will cite Arnold Schwarzenneger and Sylvester Stallone as their childhood role models.

The sufferer has a genetically inherited obsessive-compulsive disposition.

Although severe muscle dysmorphia does not yet appear to be as common as the other eating disorders, large numbers of men do seem to be unhappy with their bodies. Studies carried out in recent years have shown a growing trend in the number of men looking for ways to alter their shape. Men in their late teens seem to be particularly at risk.

When questioned in surveys, men often stated that they worked out in an attempt to build self-confidence. They felt that being 'skinny' or 'overweigh' indicated weakness. Boys who fell into either of these categories were frequently teased.

Men feel under intense pressure to attract partners and a poor body image can leave them feeling that they are not masculine enough.

In tests, it has been repeatedly shown that men believe women prefer male bodies that are 15-20 lbs. bigger than those which women actually do like. So if the majority of women are not attracted to muscular men, why do men try so hard to achieve this goal?

One argument is that since the definition of gender roles has become more indistinct, men may feel a greater need to assert themselves. Well-developed muscles separate them from women and confirm their masculinity. A strong, well-developed musculature can also make a man feel more powerful than other men.

Another growing trend is the use of muscle enhancing preparations and drugs. These can be extremely dangerous and may cause serious, long-term physical problems.

Do I have muscle dysmorphia?

If you are concerned that you may be suffering from muscle dysmorphia, try answering the following questions. If you find that you answer 'yes' to quite a few then it is recommended that you consult a doctor, since you may have a problem which requires treatment:

- ◉ Do you often worry about the shape of your body and feel that it isn't muscular enough?

- ◉ Do you study your shape by looking in the mirror more than twice a day?

- ◉ Do you constantly try to build extra muscle by frequent work-outs because you are dissatisfied with your body?

- ◉ Do you avoid social situations because they interfere with the time you spend at the gym?

- ◉ Are your work-outs starting to affect your work? Have you taken days off work or missed out on a promotion because of your exercise regime?

- ◉ Do you wear baggy clothes to hide your body? Or wear many different layers of clothing to bulk yourself up?

- ◉ Do you weigh yourself frequently?

- ◉ Do you follow special high protein/low fat diets? Have you ever bought special dietary formulas that claim to build muscle mass?

- Do you avoid visiting restaurants because it interferes with your dietary requirements and might affect your muscle tone?

- Do you try to avoid displaying your body in public (such as the beach or the gym) in case people do not think you are muscular enough?

- Do you frequently measure your body, focusing particularly on your biceps, chest or waist?

- Have you continued to work out even when you are injured? Did you feel afraid that if you stopped (even for just one day) that you would lose muscle mass and definition?

- Do you have below average body fat yet still feel unhappy with your body and general muscle size and tone?

- Do you experience mood swings or feel angry if you cannot exercise as much as you want to?

- Have you ever taken drugs such as steroids to help build up your muscles?

- Do you compare yourself to other men, worried that they are bigger than you? If you see a man who you feel is more muscular than you, does this leave you feeling depressed and envious?

If you feel that you are at risk of developing muscle dysmorphia, there are some steps you can take to help prevent the condition:

- Try not to exercise every day. Your muscles will actually develop on your 'rest' days. Make sure you take at least 2-3 days off from the gym each week.

- See if you can avoid constantly comparing yourself with other men at the gym. Remember that we are all different and have different body types. It is also important to remember that excessively muscular men may also be using dangerous methods such as steroids to build their musculature.

- Try to avoid weighing, measuring and studying your body in the mirror. It is also vital to accept that there may be minor changes to your muscle size and tone on a day-to-day basis.

- Try not to avoid social situations or cancel plans because they interfere with your work-outs. If you find this starting to happen, it is an indication that exercise is beginning to control your life.

- See if you can manage to eat a healthy, balanced diet that includes all the food groups.

- If you suffer an injury, seek medical treatment and allow your body time to heal before you begin exercising again. If you push yourself while you are injured, you risk doing serious and permanent damage to your body.

- Try to listen to what people you trust are saying. If they are complimenting you on your muscle tone, believe them. It is important to accept that even if you cannot see what they see, you still need to trust other people's judgement. Your perception of a weak, frail body are likely to be symptoms of a growing obsession and developing illness.

- If you are building muscle in an attempt to impress women, it is important to remember that many women like 'normal' or athletic bodies rather than huge muscles.

Treatment of muscle dysmorphia is still in the early stages, since it has only been recognised as a specific condition in recent years. However, specific antidepressants (such as Prozac) seem to be effective in controlling obsessive-compulsive symptoms. Behavioural therapy is often used in combination with drug therapy. **Cognitive Behavioural Therapy** can often help to modify distorted or negative thought patterns. Basic **Exposure Therapy** can also allow young men to face situations they have been avoiding in a controlled and 'safe' environment. For example, a therapist can help a sufferer to draw up a weekly plan that devotes less time to exercise and more time to socialising.

Advice for parents, carers, friends & family

It is never easy to watch and help a loved one who has an eating or exercise disorder. Often the sufferer becomes very moody, difficult and defensive when questioned about his behaviour. Family and friends may feel frustrated or even angry that their loved one cannot see the damage they are doing to themselves.

Patience and an understanding, supportive attitude are crucial if you are going to help a sufferer. Remember that your loved one is suffering from an illness and it is important to work with them against the disorder rather than against them.

If you suspect that someone you know has a problem, see if they have any of the following warning signs:

- Are they exercising for two or more hours every day?

- Do they avoid spending time with their friends or family so that they can exercise alone?

- Have they started taking dietary supplements to build body mass and muscle?

- Have they begun to develop a disproportionately large neck and shoulders?

- Are they moody and withdrawn?

- Do they seem preoccupied with their appearance and body shape?

It is important to give your loved one the time and space to talk. It may be that teasing or bullying has caused him to become self-conscious about his appearance and it may be hard for him to open up at first.

Try to listen without criticising or blaming. Encourage him to build his self-esteem by other means rather than bodybuilding. Explain the dangers of over exercising and point out that steroid use can cause long-term or permanent damage. Also encourage him to get professional help from a doctor or therapist.

Chapter 7

Body Dysmorphic Disorder

Muscle dysmorphia applies specifically to men who have issues with the size of their muscles and is a sub-category of body dysmorphic disorder. Body dysmorphic disorder refers to any problem that people have with their overall body image. Men who suffer from body dysmorphic disorder not only dislike the way they look but are obsessed with certain aspects of their appearance. These obsessions become so overpowering that they control the sufferer's life. The main concerns for sufferers appear to be hair loss, the size of their nose, genitals or muscles, any scars they might have, their skin condition and their height or weight.

Men with body dysmorphic disorder often spend hours every day checking their appearance in mirrors. They will try to disguise or cover their 'problem' areas and many will spend large sums of money on various treatments or grooming products. A growing number of men are even having plastic surgery to change their appearance.

Sufferers admit to spending up to 99% of their time focusing on their perceived flaws. This makes it very hard for them to perform well at work or enjoy social situations. They will frequently become very depressed but feel ashamed of discussing their problem, in case others think that they are just vain. They also often feel that, as men, they are supposed to be strong and so pretend that they do not have a problem.

Like people with muscle dysmorphia, sufferers of body dysmorphic disorder experience feelings of isolation, problems at work, failed relationships and some even feel so tormented that they attempt suicide.

Men seem to be becoming as focused on their appearance as women, with men's health magazines regularly promoting diet and weight loss programmes. Although it is very possible to be overweight but still fit and healthy, this idea is not usually emphasised. As men become more aware of their body image, growing numbers have developed body dysmorphic disorder. Many doctors however do not recognise the condition as yet and simply see it as low self-esteem. This is often partly due to sufferers not revealing the true extent of their problem from embarrassment.

If you feel that you may have a problem with your body image, it may be helpful to answer the following questions. If you answer 'yes' to a number of them, it would be wise to seek professional help.

Do I have body dysmorphic disorder?

- Do you worry about your appearance and spend at least an hour each day focusing on your concerns?

- Is there a particular part of your body or aspect of your appearance that really upsets you?

- Do you repeatedly check your appearance in every mirror you pass?

- Are your obsessive thoughts about your appearance affecting your work?

- Do you avoid social events because you feel too unattractive?

- Do you spend hours every day grooming and trying to camouflage your perceived flaws?

- Do you wait until it is dark before going out because then there will be fewer people around to see you?

- Have you considered surgery to correct your perceived imperfections?

- Do you feel anxious or self-conscious around other people?

- Do you pick at parts of your body or skin to try and get rid of your perceived flaws?

- Even though you may already be compulsively checking your appearance in mirrors, do you still find it difficult to look at yourself?

- Do you hide certain parts of your body?

- Do you repeatedly touch the area of your body you feel most ashamed of?

- Do you frequently compare your appearance to those of others?

- Do you exercise or diet obsessively?

- Do you hold your body in a certain position to try and hide your 'flaws' from others?

- Do you spend many hours in the bathroom each day grooming or trying to alter your appearance?

- Do you constantly ask people how you look? If they say that you look nice, do you then disregard their comments, believing that they were 'just being kind'?

- Do you argue with people when they compliment you on your appearance?

- Do you feel that people are looking at you, talking about your appearance or laughing at the way you look?

- Do you think that other people look much better than you?

- Do you try to emphasise the parts of your body you quite like, in the hope of distracting people away from the parts you feel are 'ugly'?

- Do you have difficulty looking at yourself in photographs?

- Do you put pads in your clothes to make certain areas (such as your shoulders or genitals) appear bigger?

- Do you visit dermatologists, plastic surgeons or other health professionals for appearance related treatment?

- Do you constantly measure your body?

Treating body dysmorphic disorder

A high percentage of men with body dysmorphic disorder believe that plastic surgery will be the answer to their problems. However, many find that when they approach surgeons, they are turned away because the treatment is unnecessary.

Body dysmorphic disorder can be beaten but as with eating disorders, sufferers frequently need to find expert help. Again, a combination of medication and behavioural therapy seems to be the most successful approach. As with the treatment for muscle dysmophia, certain antidepressants are very effective at controlling obsessive thoughts.

Exposure therapy can be used to help sufferers deal with their fears in a controlled way. This works especially well in situations such as social events. It is important for sufferers to take small steps forward. If they try to change too much too quickly, it can become too frightening and they may feel unable to continue.

The following is a technique which can be very helpful. Sufferers need to list all the situations that frighten them and then rank these in order, with the least frightening at the top. This scenario is then tackled first, with the sufferer practising coping in that situation until they feel comfortable enough to move onto the next stage. Other possible treatments include cognitive therapy, where the sufferer is taught how to reverse their negative thought patterns. Relaxation and breathing techniques can also help sufferers deal with panic attacks.

Affirmations and visualisations may feel trivial or even pointless at first but it is worth persevering with them since they can help a great deal. It is important to remember that if a person constantly repeats negative thoughts, this will eventually lead to negative feelings and low self-esteem. Therefore, if they can learn to repeat positive affirmations, they will gradually begin to feel better about themselves. Massage can also help sufferers to feel more in touch with their body. Initially, it may be difficult for them to allow a stranger to touch their body but again, perseverance can lead to very positive results.

It is also extremely important for sufferers to discover why their illness developed in the first place. Often it can be due to childhood teasing from peers or relatives. Another problem is that men are becoming increasingly affected by strong media messages about the 'ideal' body shape and size. Try to accept that being happy is not about having a 'flawless' complexion or a 'perfect' appearance. Remember that this is just the outside packaging and it is what is inside that really counts.

In addition, it is very important to understand that (as with eating disorders) body dysmorphic disorder usually develops because of emotional or psychological problems. Having surgery to alter a person's appearance to one that is 'perfect' will not solve the underlying problems or issues. This is why it is very important to seek professional help to get to the root of the problem. Deeper feelings of self-loathing, insecurity, inferiority and fear of failure are hidden by the body dysmorphic disorder or muscle dysmorphia. It is these problems though which really need to be addressed.

Chapter 8

Men And Their Emotions

Eating disorders in men (as in women) are not about food or vanity. They develop as a way of coping with difficult feelings, pressures from work or home and the stresses of life when it feels out of control. Men can turn to an eating disorder because they feel that their food intake is something which they can control. The key to preventing eating disorders and food related problems is by talking about feelings and emotions.

However, talking about feelings is something that men traditionally find very difficult. Men do not usually enter therapy due to a need to talk but because they are forced into counselling by a partner or work colleague when their behaviour is seen as being out of control. Traditionally, men do not like to ask for help in any aspect of their lives. When lost in a new town, women will frequently stop their car and ask for directions. However, men are much more likely to consult maps, continue driving around until they find a useful road sign or allow their passengers to ask for directions instead.

Why do men find it difficult to ask for help?

There are a number of reasons why men struggle to allow others to help them and these are linked to certain key male characteristics:

Shame

Men often feel that asking for support and advice makes them appear weak or foolish. This is very ironic since it is in fact the strongest and bravest people who are the ones that can reach out and ask for help when they need it. However, it is this shame about their own perceived 'weaknesses' which lead men to cover up their feelings and emotions. As mentioned earlier, most men are brought up with the idea that 'boys don't cry'. It is considered to be effeminate if they shed tears when they are feeling sad or hurt. The following letter from a men's health magazine demonstrates this point perfectly:

> "I know that men are supposed to cry too and a lot of people seem to think it helps but I think it's the start of a slippery slope to emotional chaos. I never shed a tear when my wife passed - it wouldn't have helped her and I didn't think it would have helped me. Be strong, hold back the tears, keep your emotions under control and you'll be a stronger person for yourself and those around you."

Unfortunately, 'being strong' is not the way to deal with difficult emotions. Repression is a method that men frequently use but it usually leads to long-term problems. Our feelings cannot be repressed forever and they begin to show in other ways. Men often become angry when they are dealing with difficult emotions.

When a man is struggling with a particular feeling of shame or inadequacy, he is likely to project this onto someone else – usually a partner or loved one. For example, if a man feels he is overweight or is conscious about any aspect of his appearance, he may start criticising his partner's looks instead. Again, eating disorder sufferers are much more likely to adopt the more feminine approach and criticise their own looks rather than someone else's.

Long term repression of feelings can lead to problems such as eating disorders, drink or drug related issues and/or depression. When a man has repressed serious issues such as bullying since childhood, this can begin to cause major illnesses in later life.

Unfortunately, parents often pass on their negative feelings and attitudes to their children. Fathers may be worried their sons will not be tough enough if they express their feelings by crying. A father may fear that his son will be teased or called a 'sissy' if he cries at school. However, this attitude means that men not only grow up unable to deal with their own emotions but also struggle when faced with women's feelings.

When they see a woman crying, men usually want to 'fix' the problem. Instead of simply listening to the problem and responding with sympathy and understanding, men want to find an instant solution. If that is not possible and they cannot immediately solve the problem then they become frustrated. This leads them to become snappy and difficult, which in turn upsets the woman, who begins to wish that she hadn't shared her problem in the first place.

The best way to remedy this is for the man to learn how to deal with his uncomfortable feelings, even though they may make him feel vulnerable. It is not easy for a man to watch someone he cares about cry, and finding an answer to her problem seems like the ideal solution. Ironically though, she is likely to feel better if she is allowed to talk through all her painful emotions and is just given a sympathetic and understanding response.

Another way in which men exhibit shame about their feelings is to talk in half sentences. They will leave a brief clue about how they feel by bringing up a subject and then hoping that someone will question them further and draw out the truth. For example, a friend who has been recently divorced and is now having serious self-esteem issues said, "I saw a beautiful woman at work today." This was actually shorthand for, "I saw a beautiful woman at work today and thought that she would never like me. I think that I'm ugly and fat and will never be in a relationship again."

Although men do not express their emotions and insecurities in the same way that women do, similar feelings are still bubbling away beneath the surface. However, it is generally only difficult feelings that men relate in half sentences because they feel ashamed. If they have had some good news, this is often expressed immediately and at great length since it makes them feel proud and strong. They feel like powerful and worthy men, who have achieved success.

Men will often try to minimise any shame they feel by using different coping mechanisms, such as:

- Covering it with anger.

- Becoming silent and uncommunicative.

- Growing defensive and monosyllabic.

- Lying.

- Becoming evasive and changing the subject.

- Covering it with humour.

However, men are not just trying to cover up the shame that they feel. They are also trying to bury all the painful feelings which caused the shame to develop in the first place.

Frequently, men only seem to feel uncomfortable with emotions that leave them feeling vulnerable. Most men are happy to express real anger since this can leave them feeling powerful and in charge of a situation (although this is not usually true for eating disorder sufferers). When they have exhausted all their options for dealing with shame and none of them have worked though, men often blame their feelings on others.

Women usually attribute their success to others but accept the blame for any failure themselves. However, men tend to be very proud of their successes and attribute them to their own hard work whilst often blaming others for their failures. At this point, men with eating disorders (especially anorexia) deviate from typical male behaviour patterns. They are far more likely to accept the more feminine trait and blame themselves for any problems.

As mentioned earlier, therapy is an area which men try very hard to avoid. They usually feel tremendous shame when accepting counselling and believe that they will be rejected by other men and seen as 'weak'. Instead, they will often battle on with their problems rather than seek help. This then results in their problem developing further and in the case of an eating disorder, it can frequently become acute. Men usually only come forwards for help when their condition is so bad that they have serious physical complications.

Men try very hard to prevent others from discovering their true feelings and struggle to bury them, even from themselves. Yet when they actually do open up, the response they get is usually very supportive. Most people respond with care and understanding, and in turn then feel safe enough to share their own experiences. Even just acknowledging the feeling of shame is a good start and opens up communication.

This is demonstrated very clearly in the following responses the letter writer received in the male health magazine to his comments about crying. He was shown empathy, understanding and encouragement, as well as being given the strong message that it is vital to express difficult feelings:

- "Cry at the earliest possible opportunity. Forget all that macho rubbish and let the emotion out - bottling it up does you no favours… Don't feel ashamed to express your grief. It's normal. It's the ones who tell you not to cry who really have the problem."

- "Don't be too proud to accept help – especially from those trained to give it. My daughter was diagnosed with terminal cancer a year ago and I just couldn't believe it was true. It wasn't until I saw one of the grief counsellors at the hospital that I was able to start accepting things."

- "Have counselling. It's that simple. Having coped with a death in my family twice now, the second time I decided I needed to talk to someone unconnected with me. Counselling is about learning to express yourself without feeling embarrassed. Believe me, it was a massive help."

- "Don't be too proud to open up, and don't try and kid yourself that you don't need a friend to talk to. When my wife died I thought the bottom had dropped out of my world. I couldn't believe any of the friends and family offering to help me could do anything at all to make me feel better. But knowing what I know now I wish I'd taken the opportunity to talk to them sooner…"

Avoidance

Men often try to avoid thinking about their emotions. When asked a direct question about how they are feeling, they frequently reply with the stock answer of 'fine' or a quick 'I don't know'. Alternatively, they turn the question around and try to intellectualise it. This means that they can respond with thoughts rather than feelings. For example, their sentences are likely to begin, "I think..." rather than, "I feel..."

When dealing with the death of a friend, women will typically express a whole range of emotions. They will describe their feelings for the friend and show their sadness through tears. Men are more likely to think about how it affects them and will start wondering about their own mortality and the meaning life. This allows them to completely avoid looking at how they actually feel about the loss of their friend.

By avoiding their emotions, men can make themselves feel almost invulnerable. If they repress any feelings of fear or anxiety, this allows them to take huge risks. This is vital in certain jobs such as high finance, where the men who deny that they have any nerves are able to take the biggest risks and secure the best promotions. However, denying their emotions can lead men to become insensitive to others. Also, by 'switching off' their sense of fear, men often allow themselves to enter very hazardous situations such as war zones.

However, our feelings of fear are there as a warning system to protect us against these dangerous situations. Due to the way our society has developed though, men are sometimes expected to suppress their fears and be heroic whilst at other times they are encouraged to express these fears and make themselves more approachable. It is not surprising therefore that men often suffer from confusion as to exactly how they should behave at times.

When men avoid discussing or looking at their feelings, this can result in them growing remote or emotionally absent. If a person is numb to their own feelings, they are far more likely to be unaware of the feelings of the people around them. They are then likely to be seen as 'uncaring'.

Men tend to act on their emotions by carrying out an action. Rather than deal with their feelings about a certain situation, they prefer to alter that situation. This is demonstrated clearly in men with muscle dysmorphia. Instead of learning to cope with their negative feelings about their body and addressing the reasons why these developed, they strive to alter their bodies instead. This is in the belief that by changing their body into the 'perfect shape' they will solve all these problems.

Insecurity

Men are still expected to be strong providers in our society. A man who does not work or who does not look after his family is often looked down on and even classed as a failure. However, men also feel a need to be looked after and cared for rather than simply always being the provider or protector.

This is another reason why eating disorders can develop. Young adults may find their expected roles in society simply too frightening and intimidating. The responsibilities that a young adult male has to take on may seem too daunting and the eating disorder offers an 'escape route' back into the security and safety of their childhood.

The fact that all men, at times, feel the need to be nurtured goes against the entire basis of the macho male image. This means that men often react to these feelings by trying to adopt an even stronger masculine image.

It seems that men in general are afraid of being seen as feminine. They are frightened of showing their female side by exhibiting tenderness or discussing their emotions. When in groups, they will often talk about women purely in terms of their anatomy, viewing them only as objects. They will also try to avoid becoming 'trapped' in what they feel is an emotionally stifling relationship.

This fear of being seen as feminine extends to eating disorder sufferers and is one of the reasons why men feel afraid of admitting to their disorder. Anorexia and bulimia are seen as 'women's illnesses' and men are frequently afraid that they will be seen as feminine if they talk openly about their problems.

Men are often afraid that behaving in a 'feminine' manner will lead to them being thought of as gay. Again, this fear extends to male eating disorder sufferers, who may be afraid of being labelled as homosexual if they admit to their problems.

In the last 100 years, the role of women has radically changed in our society and this seems to have added to the levels of male insecurity. In the past, male and female roles were more clearly defined. Men were usually in charge of the thinking and actions - i.e. they went out to work to bring home enough money to feed and clothe their family, and they made all the important family decisions. By contrast, women were responsible for looking after the emotional well being of the family.

Today, these roles have altered dramatically. Women are often powerful, assertive, driven and goal orientated while men can be sensitive, understanding, supportive and emotionally open. In many cases, there has been a complete role reversal in couples. The woman may be very dominant, controlling and demanding (traditionally the more typical male role) while the man might be passive, caring and spend his time trying to please his partner. I have seen numerous examples of this type of relationship, where the children seek kindness and nurturing from their father when they are hurt or upset.

This kind of dominant/passive relationship is unhealthy whichever roles the partners play. For a relationship to work properly, both partners need to accept that they have both 'male' and 'female' characteristics. Unfortunately, it is often very hard for men to accept that they have any feminine aspects and respond instead by reasserting their masculinity even more strongly.

Aggressive Behaviour

Anger and aggression are natural traits in everyone. However, they do seem to be more fully defined in men and may be used as a response to feelings of insecurity. Men need to be seen as strong and powerful, and often fight each other in order to prove supremacy. All men need to show some aggression but when it is continuous or inappropriate, problems can arise.

In the case of eating disorder sufferers, any anger they feel has been turned in on themselves. Unable to deal with conflicting emotions, they have turned these inwards and choose to punish their own body instead. This can also be seen with people who self-harm. Unable to deal with a situation that involves conflict, they will remain passive but injure themselves when they are alone. We all need to learn how to deal with our anger in a healthy, non-destructive manner.

It is important that men are allowed to show some aggression but it must not be overpowering. If they are met with another person's aggression when they become angry, this is more likely to temper their behaviour. However, it is also very important to disarm aggression with care and affection, and this is especially important with eating disorder sufferers. They have turned their aggression so completely inwards that any care and nurturing is rejected in favour of anger and punishment.

When a person is unable to express their anger, this can lead to self-destructive behaviour. Depriving yourself can also be a way of getting back at another person. This may be on a subconscious level, since many eating disorder sufferers feel that they only want to hurt themselves. However, it may also be a conscious decision, as in the case of a young man in a difficult relationship who had reached the point of planning his own suicide. He commented that, "If I kill myself, that will show my wife. That will finally make her hurt in the way that she's hurt me."

Self-destructive behaviour is another way of demonstrating aggression and it can be very difficult to help someone who has taken on this role. Being a 'failure' or adopting a 'sick role' (in the case of many eating disorder sufferers) becomes their identity. They need to behave in this way if they are to gain the sympathy, support and nurturing they crave.

Trying to 'rescue' someone with self-destructive tendencies can just reinforce this role since they see that their negative behaviour is attracting the attention they desperately need. Instead, it is important to help the sufferer discover why they need to be a 'failure' or a 'sick' person. This again involves talking about feelings, which is often very difficult and will be one of the reasons why the sufferer turned to their behaviour in the first place.

I know that when I was suffering from anorexia, I felt unable to talk about my feelings or the abuse and bullying I had suffered throughout my childhood. I was showing my internal pain through my self-destructive behaviour instead. My thinness was an indication that there was something very wrong and that I needed help to talk about my feelings and emotions.

The male ego

Simply knowing that they are male is not usually enough for most men. They often feel compelled to continually prove it to themselves through their achievements. They need to feel strong and powerful, and to gain recognition for this. This need to constantly prove himself can leave a man feeling very alone. For example, if a man immerses himself in his work, this can be to the total exclusion of his friends and family.

Men frequently try to build their self-esteem by accumulating wealth and power, although this may be a response to other problems in their life. If a man feels badly about his appearance for instance, he may try and surround himself with status symbols to help boost his esteem. In young men, these could be sports cars and designer clothes whereas for teenage boys it might be the latest music or games systems. These material goods are only short-term distractions from the real problem though. Again, talking through the issues which have led to the low self-esteem is the vital factor.

At times, we can all channel our energies into different areas of our life to avoid looking at the real issues. Men who have experienced problems at home can find themselves trying to disappear into their work. A man who was experiencing serious marital problems found that they had left him feeling emasculated. In response, his work began to take on a vital importance and his workmates became his surrogate family. As a result, the distress he felt when one of his new 'family' was unhappy or behaved badly was out of all proportion to the actual problem. He would become depressed and frequently stopped eating as a way of punishing himself for 'failing' his team. It was only when he finally started to talk about his feelings and his home life that he began to see the link with his behaviour at work.

As has been shown throughout this chapter, talking openly about feelings and emotions with someone you trust is the key to good mental health. However, it is unusual for men to be this emotionally open and honest for many of the reasons just shown.

Culture and family background are also contributing factors in a man's character. Our parents are also very important influences on our lives. If a man's father is emotionally very withdrawn and doesn't discuss his feelings, his son may well grow up with similar attitudes.

In addition, the sexes of other family members can be important and play a key role in defining a young man's character. If a boy grows up with only brothers as siblings then the atmosphere is more likely to be quite competitive and aggressive. Even the mother may find herself losing some of her softer feminine qualities. Whereas in a family which is predominantly female, the son may find himself adapting to the gentler, more open and caring atmosphere, and developing his feminine side.

There are exceptions to these examples though. In a family where the daughters are all girls and the parents desperately want a boy, if they do have a son he may respond by strongly developing his masculine traits to please his parents.

Similarly, in a family where there are two or three boys, the parents are more likely to want a girl. If their next child is a boy again, he may respond to their wishes by developing a quieter, sensitive feminine nature. However, this blurring of the gender roles can create problems and may lead to teasing, both at school and at home. This can cause many of the classic male insecurities to begin and again may lead to the development of an eating disorder.

Chapter 9

Men & Depression

Depression is one of the most common symptoms of an eating disorder. As an illness in it's own right though, it still remains unclear whether depression triggers an eating disorder or vice versa. Either way, the two conditions are closely linked. It is estimated that at least three-quarters of all eating disorder sufferers experience some form of serious depression.

However, as men frequently find it hard to admit that they are suffering from depression, this makes treating the condition difficult. Medical treatment for depression is often an essential part of the overall treatment for eating disorders. Often, it is vital for a sufferer to feel mentally 'brighter' before they can tackle the other symptoms and root causes of their illness.

If you suspect that you may be suffering from depression, try answering the following list of questions. If you answer 'yes' to a number of them (and you have felt that way for two weeks or more) it would be very wise to seek medical help:

- Do you feel irritable and find yourself snapping at people?

- Are you overwhelmed by negative feelings?

- Do you feel tired all the time?

- Are you having trouble sleeping?

- Have your eating habits changed? Do you find yourself eating too much or too little?

- Do you find it hard to cope with any criticism?

- Are you becoming withdrawn and avoid spending time with friends or family?

- Do you feel anxious and restless much of the time?

- Have you suffered any panic attacks?

- Do you feel that you are lacking in confidence?

- Do you feel worthless or a failure?

- Does your life feel hopeless?

- Do you have trouble concentrating?

- Do you find that you no longer enjoy the things that you used to?

- Have you had suicidal thoughts?

- Are your energy levels low much of the time?

- Have you experienced any difficult, frightening or painful memories from the past?

- Do you have difficulty making decisions and find yourself relying on others to help you?

- Have you carried out any of the following behaviours because you felt desperate:

  - Drinking or taking drugs.
  - Long periods of absence from school or work.
  - Self-harming.
  - Becoming violent or suffering from uncontrollable rage.
  - Lying, cheating or stealing.

Often, men feel that depression is another 'women's illness' and are too ashamed to ask for help. However, recent studies have shown that men are just as vulnerable to depression as women and are actually more likely to commit suicide.

Men tend to see depression as an 'emotional' illness and are afraid of being labelled as 'weak' or 'crazy' if they admit to these feelings. Instead, they try to find physical causes for their problems. For example, if they awaken frequently in the night sweating heavily and suffering from a churning stomach, they will tend to put this down to a stomach upset. In actual fact, the likelihood is that this is one of a number of symptoms of depression that they are suffering from and not recognising.

Men and women often show the symptoms of depression in different ways. Women are more likely to cry or blame themselves for every problem whereas men tend to become aggressive or even violent. They may turn to drink to ease their depressive feelings and this can lead to a misdiagnosis of the problem.

Fear of possible treatment methods can also stop some men from admitting to their problem. The media often overemphasise extreme treatments, such as electric shock therapy or the use of strong medications, and this can intimidate sufferers.

Often, concern or fear can lead people to react inappropriately. Comments from family or friends who do not understand the complex nature of depression (such as, "Why don't you just pull yourself together?") are not helpful to sufferers, who are already ashamed of their condition.

There is a popular myth that strong willpower can beat depression and this is likely to make a severely depressed man feel total despair. This myth puts forward the idea that depression is a choice and that sufferers are simply using the illness as a way of hurting others. In reality, depression is frequently triggered by a chemical imbalance in the brain and medical treatment is essential for recovery.

Although it is dependent on the nature of the depression, lifestyle changes and a positive mental attitude can often alleviate some of the symptoms. Talking is another vital part of recovery but again, this is often something men find very difficult. Also, if they meet any amount of hostility or disapproval when they are open and honest about their feelings, this can leave them feeling rejected and vulnerable. As a result, they are less likely to openly discuss their feelings in the future and by 'bottling up' these emotions, this can lead to serious problems.

In addition, some men are afraid that if they start getting help for their depression, they will become addicted to that help. Men often feel that if they start talking, they won't be able to stop. They are worried that they will lose their ability to control, deny or block their feelings. However, the purpose of treatment is to actually give control back to the sufferer.

Depression is a very individual illness and the symptoms vary in every case. The term 'depression' covers a huge variety of symptoms, and ranges in severity from temporary unhappiness to suicidal despair.

Men are also starting to make different life choices. They are beginning to share many predominantly female concerns, such as if and when they should have children. Fears about 'time running out' and approaching middle age can cause depression in men even in their twenties.

Appearance related depression amongst men is also now far more common. For teenage boys and younger men, concerns about their height, weight, skin, muscle tone or genital development may also bring on serious depression.

Depression is quite a common illness for men and some of the most productive and creative men throughout history have been sufferers. Frequently, they believe that their creative powers actually come from their painful feelings and emotions, and are afraid that they will lose their artistic talents if they achieve happiness. As a result, they may actually begin to feel dependent on their illness.

Some famous men who have suffered from clinical depression include Samuel Coleridge (poet), Abraham Lincoln (U.S. President), Winston Churchill (British Prime Minister), Rembrandt (artist), Spike Milligan and John Cleese (comedians), Rod Steiger (actor), Kurt Cobain (musician) and Ernest Hemingway and Mark Twain (writers).

The difference between depression and unhappiness

It is natural for everyone to experience periods of sadness in their life. These are the result of particular events such as the death of a loved one or problems at home, work or school. When sadness is linked to a particular event, it only lasts for a limited period of time. However, if the feelings persist and begin to cause other problems then it is time to seek help. If a man is unable to deal with his temporary sadness in a healthy manner (such as by talking through his feelings and emotions) then it is far more likely that other problems will develop. Often, men will avoid dealing with different feelings and try to focus on something else altogether instead.

Although talking about different feelings and emotions is an essential part of recovery, it is important not to focus on these solely. If you are constantly thinking about how bad you feel and are calling yourself a failure, the depression will only deepen. It is very important to remember that negative thoughts lead to negative feelings. Constant worrying and obsessing can be very dangerous.

What does depression feel like?

When someone is experiencing feelings of sadness, they are still able to ask for help and support. They are also able to ease their own pain in various different ways. With depression though, the sufferer feels totally trapped and is unable to find anything that will comfort them or ease their pain. They often feel unable to let anyone help and may push away those closest to them. This overwhelming sense of bleakness and hopelessness is continuous and generally lasts for weeks or months.

Often, depression is described as 'blackness'. When I was suffering from the condition, I would talk of feeling trapped in a black pit that had impossibly high walls with smooth sides, which I was unable to climb. The following are a selection of quotes from other sufferers, describing their depression.

"A living death, which robs everything of meaning or purpose. I feel numb."

"A gradual shutting out of all light."

"It was like an all consuming dark swamp that took over my life."

When talking to the **psychiatrist** Antony Clare, Spike Milligan described his depression as follows:

"It is like every fibre in your body is screaming for relief, yet there is no relief... The whole world is taken away and all there is, is this black void, this terrible, terrible, empty, aching black void."

Winston Churchill also spoke of being haunted by the 'black dog' of depression.

When a person feels depressed, they usually cannot see any brightness in their life - all they see is bleakness, pain, destruction, misery and suffering. They lose the ability to feel any emotion strongly and their vitality disappears. As well as feeling drained, they often believe that they are a burden to others. This is why suicide can seem like the solution to all their problems. The number of deaths from suicide does seem to be increasing, especially in the 15-19 age group. This again demonstrates how vital it is that young men learn to talk about their feelings and problems. It has been reported that the number of deaths from suicide in the UK is approximately the same as the number of AIDS related deaths.

Depression is not just an illness of adult men though. Research has indicated that around 10% of children under the age of 12 have suffered from a depressive episode. The teen years are also a time when young men are susceptible to bouts of depression.

What causes depression?

There has been a great deal of continuing research into this disorder. As with eating disorders, many different factors are involved in triggering depression. These may be genetic, biochemical, psychological and environmental:

Genetic

Depression does appear to run in families and some Canadian researchers claim that a faulty gene affecting **serotonin** levels is associated with depression.

Biochemical

Other researchers believe that depression is linked to problems with the endocrine system, which controls the function of hormones in the body. Another theory is that depression is the result of improperly functioning neurotransmitters. Neurotransmitters are chemical messengers that transmit signals between nerve cells and which control feelings, thoughts and behaviours. Depression is thought to be connected with two specific neurotransmitters - serotonin and norepinephrine.

Psychological and Environmental

Major stresses can trigger eating disorders and they can also cause depression to develop. Too much stress can upset the balance and functioning of neurotransmitters. This stress can be both negative (illness, divorce, the death of a loved one, etc.) or positive (moving house, school or job). Other stresses which can lead to depression include - bullying, health problems, homelessness, money issues, alcohol or drug abuse, unemployment, natural disasters and sexual problems (including very serious issues such as rape). Any of these events can potentially trigger depression and/or eating problems.

How depression affects your health

Depression affects the body in many different ways and it can lead to further health problems. When a person is suffering from depression, they begin to neglect their body. They may stop their daily washing routine, forget to change their clothes and neglect their diet. They might also find that they have no appetite and stop eating, or alternatively they may crave high fat / high sugar foods. As a result, their diet becomes deficient in essential nutrients, which affects their mood even further.

Depressed men often experience feelings of anger. They find that they react with irrational bursts of rage when faced with any irritant. This is a major health concern since research has shown that men who frequently lose their temper are three times more likely to have a heart attack then those who are able to remain calm.

Depression can lead a man to completely withdraw from day to day life. Some sufferers take to their bed because life has just become too daunting a prospect. However, there are treatments available for depression, which are extremely effective. There are also a number of steps that sufferers can take to help themselves feel better.

Treating depression

- ◉ **Recognise that you need help.** It is not always easy to accept that we need help and sometimes it is comments from a friend or loved one which can be the trigger for finding support.

- ◉ **Visit your doctor.** They may prescribe antidepressants and/or suggest that you see a therapist.

- ◉ **Seek out support groups or telephone helplines.** Depression is an illness which can require help at any hour of the day or night. Always try to have telephone helpline numbers (such as The Samaritans) to hand, which you can phone if you are feeling desperate. Support groups can also be excellent sources of help. They meet regularly at private houses or in local halls, depending on the size of the group.

- **Learn more about the condition.** Information leaflets from your local surgery, TV programmes and books can all help to teach you more about your illness. A lot of the fears we have come from a lack of knowledge and so the more you can find out about your illness, the less frightening it will seem.

- **List the factors which led to your depression.** For example, job loss, exam failure or financial problems, and then take some action to alter the situation.

- **Keep reminding yourself that depression is treatable.** It is very important not to lose hope.

- **Try to have more fun.** Even though you may not feel motivated to "have fun", try and spend at least one hour each day doing an activity you enjoy.

- **Healthy exercise can help to lift a low mood.** Although it is still uncertain whether exercise has any lasting effect on severe depression, it is very important. Often, when a person feels depressed, they lack energy and motivation. Gentle walking on a daily basis is vital in keeping the body functioning properly.

- **Follow a healthy diet.** This is to reduce the risk of suffering from any deficiencies.

- **Try to accept yourself for who you are.** The majority of men are constantly striving to achieve by competing with others. It is important to accept that, as a man, you also have needs and require comfort and support.

Antidepressants

Antidepressants are not addictive and are effective in between 80-90% of cases. They help to relieve feelings of hopelessness and despair, as well as treating other symptoms such as **insomnia**, anxiety and fatigue. Usually, these medications need to be taken for 2-3 weeks before the sufferer notices any change in their mood. This is because it takes a while for the drug to reach the correct level in the bloodstream.

It is also very important to keep taking the prescribed dose, even when your mood has lifted. Doctors generally recommend that patients continue taking their medication for between 4 and 12 months after their depressive symptoms have lifted. There are a number of side effects associated with antidepressants and unfortunately, these often appear before the sufferer feels any lifting of their mood. This can lead some people to give up on their medication before they have given it a chance. Perseverance is important when treating depression since not all antidepressants suit everyone. Sometimes, doctors have to try a few different types before they find the correct one for their patient.

Therapy

Broadly speaking, psychotherapy means 'talking cure'. Therapy is therefore basically all about a client talking through their problems with a therapist. It is very important that you find a recommended therapist, who is well trained and respected in their field. It is also very important that the client/therapist relationship is good and the sufferer feels able to talk openly about their personal issues. If you are considering therapy, talk first with your doctor, as they are likely to be able to refer you to a recommended therapist. If you are choosing a private therapist, the following questions are important ones to ask before you make a commitment:

- What code of ethics does the therapist follow and which professional bodies are they accountable to? This is important because it shows that the therapist is fully qualified and registered with the correct medical authorities.

- Does the therapist have professional supervision? This is essential for all practising therapists. A supervisor oversees their work, provides constructive feedback and checks that no problems are developing.

- What is the therapist's style of counselling and which types of therapy do they offer their clients?

- Does the therapist have a referral system if they feel that they need extra help?

- Do they have a 'contract' system whereby a client signs up for a set number of sessions?

It may be that you need to try a number of different therapists before you find one who you feel comfortable with and who provides you with the level of support that you need.

Many of the points mentioned in this chapter work equally well for eating disorder sufferers, which again shows how the two illnesses are closely linked. Above all, perseverance is essential with both conditions. Recovery from depression is likely to take some time but with the correct level of support and treatment, a full recovery is very possible.

Chapter 10

Eating Disorders & Homosexuality

Another myth concerning eating disorders is that all male sufferers are homosexual. This idea has caused many heterosexual sufferers to avoid treatment in case they are considered gay. However, although gay men do seem to have an increased risk of developing an eating disorder, statistics show that only 20% of male sufferers are homosexual.

As mentioned previously, studies of male anorexics have shown that many sufferers lack assertive masculinity. They seem to exhibit more feminine qualities such as sensitivity, guilt, sadness and be more emotionally expressive. This may be due to a strong female role model in their life and does not automatically mean that they are or will become homosexual.

Many gay men do feel that their culture often places a lot of emphasis on looking good and this can lead them to search for extreme methods of altering their appearance.

A comment by the pop singer George Michael showed how important size can be to gay men. Discussing events after his arrest in a US lavatory for lewd behaviour, he said, "The most horrific thing that happened was that I was photographed with my shirt off and I was fat. Can you imagine two worse things than being fat and gay?"

However, as with women, eating disorders usually develop for a number of different reasons. These can relate to the stresses in a person's life, low self-esteem, problems from their past and/or depression.

Unfortunately, our society is still often very critical of homosexuality. If gay men feel rejected by their friends and family because of their sexuality, this can cause their self-esteem to drop, which may lead to eating problems developing.

In recent years, our society has begun to place more emphasis on the appearance of men. For heterosexual men, this seems to focus more on gaining weight and developing muscles. They try to build and tone their physique so that it becomes sculptured. However, this can often lead to problems such as muscle dysmorphia.

In contrast, the gay community generally places more emphasis on a 'slim' body as the ideal. Like most women, gay men will often mistakenly believe themselves to be overweight. This can then lead them to begin dieting and an eating disorder may develop.

However, there have been some general cultural changes within the gay community recently. Whereas previously, the 'ideal' body shape for homosexual men was generally **ectomorphic** (tall and thin), the spread of AIDS has begun to bring about a change. The ravaging effects that AIDS has on the body have led to the idea that a **mesomorphic** figure (sturdy and muscular) may be more desirable.

Eating disorders are often caused by problematic relationships, either during childhood or in adult life. Overeating and restricting can be a way of 'dealing' with relationship stresses. Losing or gaining weight may be a subconscious attempt by a person to make themselves appear unattractive to the people around them. This then means that they are 'safe' from the problems associated with a new relationship.

Teenage boys usually struggle with the new sexual feelings that they are experiencing. If they find that they are developing homosexual feelings, this can often be an added pressure for them. **Internalising** negative social messages about homosexuality can cause serious self-image problems and this can lead to further problems.

Some young men discover that they can reduce their sexual drive through starvation, allowing them to temporarily escape from their confusing sexual feelings. Fear of their family's reaction may lead them to feel that it is preferable to cover their feelings with an eating disorder rather than admit to their homosexuality.

Research has shown that as well as suffering from eating disorders, there are also higher incidences of depression amongst gay men. This could be due to the lack of acceptance towards homosexuality in our society. Gay men are often unfairly made to feel ashamed of their sexuality and are treated like second-class citizens.

Although there have been a number of studies carried out in this area, the statistics are unfortunately still limited and the size of studies very small. In 2002, the Department of Psychology at Harvard, recruited 122 men between the ages of 18 and 50. Of these men, 64 were heterosexual and 58 were homosexual. The homosexual men reported higher levels of depression, disordered eating and feelings of discomfort about their sexual orientation. None of the heterosexual men suffered from bulimia compared to eight of the gay men. Similarly, twelve homosexual men were anorexic compared to only one of the heterosexual men.

Unfortunately, there do not seem to be many eating disorder support groups specifically for homosexual men. This means that they have to join other support groups and can find that they are the only gay man present, which can isolate them further. However, it is very important that sufferers do not allow this to deter them from reaching out for support.

Part Two

Recovering From An Eating Disorder

Chapter 11

Treatment

Treatment for many less serious weight and exercise issues can often be undertaken without professional assistance. However, conditions such as eating disorders and exercise related problems (including muscle dysmorphia) will require expert help. Men who suffer from obesity or compulsive overeating may also need structured help from professionals such as **dieticians** or nutritionists.

It is very important that anyone who decides to change their diet dramatically for whatever reason should have a check-up with their doctor first to ensure that this is safe for them.

When a person's day-to-day life is constantly affected by their negative behaviour then it is time for them to seek out help. Men often feel afraid to reveal that they have food or weight related issues. This is underlined by the fact that the number of men admitting to having food related problems rises dramatically when there is some sympathetic publicity about men and eating disorders. However, there are currently many different kinds of help available and it is very important that men find the courage to seek out that support.

Most eating disorder programmes are geared towards out-patient treatment. It is only in extreme cases that in-patient treatment is recommended. Very occasionally, sufferers are forced to accept treatment because they are a danger to themselves and can be taken into hospital on a section (under the UK Mental Health Act 1983).

When you decide that you would like to start recovering from your eating disorder, the first step should be to visit your family doctor. There might be a number of reasons why you feel it is time for you to attempt recovery. You may be suffering many physical problems. You may have tried to recover by yourself but found it too hard. You may feel pressured by the constant comments of friends or family. Alternatively, you may just feel that you are losing your life to the eating disorder. Whatever the reason, seeking help is a very wise and brave step.

You might feel very nervous about visiting your doctor for the first time, so consider taking a friend or relative along for moral support. You may also be afraid that you will feel initimidated and not talk honestly about your problems. Try writing a list of all that you want to tell the doctor and refer to this during the appointment if your mind goes blank.

If you have been suffering from an eating disorder for a number of years, your doctor is likely to want to check how you are physically. S/he may send you for blood tests, an ECG (to check the condition of your heart) and possibly a Dexa Scan to test bone density. S/he is also likely to want to measure your weight. This may feel intrusive but it is an important indication of your state of health.

Some eating disorder specialists advise weighing a sufferer backwards so that they cannot see the reading on the scale. This may be helpful for some sufferers (I know that I found it beneficial) and you might want to mention this idea to your doctor.

Unfortunately, not all family doctors completely understand eating disorders. There is a slight chance that the first doctor you see may not take your problem as seriously as they should. If this is the case, it is very important not to give up. Most surgeries have more than one doctor and so make another appointment and try again.

Your doctor might suggest a number of different treatment options and these are likely to depend on your physical state. If you are dangerously underweight then it is possible that a stay at an in-patient specialist unit is necessary.

However, most treatment programmes are on an out-patient basis and it is likely that you will be referred to one of these. There are many different medical professionals who can help with recovery, including psychiatrists, **psychologists**, eating disorder specialists, dieticians, community psychiatric nurses, occupational therapists and **counsellors**.

It is always important to find a therapist that you can relate to. This may mean that you need to visit more than one before you connect and feel comfortable talking openly about your problems. Again, try to be patient and not give up if you do not connect with the first therapist you visit.

For a good working relationship between the therapist and sufferer, it is important that the sufferer feels able to state what they feel they need from treatment. It is vital that carers, friends and family also listen to the sufferer's thoughts, even if they do not always agree with them. For much of their life, a sufferer has had difficulty expressing their feelings and it is very important to encourage openness and honesty.

During an initial treatment assessment, it is also important for the sufferer to ask questions and discuss all of their fears and concerns about treatment, even if they feel these are irrational. Their fears may relate to weight gain and the thought of 'ballooning in size' when they start to eat a normal diet again or to fears of how they will cope without the eating disorder as their 'escape route'. A trained medical profession will be able to address all of these matters before and during treatment.

It may be that you are referred to see a Community Psychiatric Nurse (CPN) who can help you to alter your diet, check on your physical progress and also teach therapies such as CBT (Cognitive Behavioural Therapy). CBT is now one of the preferred methods of treatment for eating disorders (as stated in the UK NICE Guidelines for Eating Disorders 2004). If you begin this form of therapy, either for bulimia or anorexia, treatment will probably last for between 16 and 20 sessions (4 to 6 months).

CBT is based on the idea that that our thoughts affect our feelings. Therefore, if we think negative thoughts we are likely to feel depressed. By contrast, if we can think more positively we are likely to feel brighter. For eating disorder sufferers this means that if they are constantly thinking negatively about their body, they are likely to feel unhappy.

Usually, eating disorder sufferers do not only focus negatively on their body but on many different aspects of their life. They frequently believe themselves to be failures at their work as well. When I had learnt the basis of Cognitive Therapy, my CPN gave me a list of questions to ask myself whenever my head was filled with negative thoughts. These were:

◉   What are the facts? Are my thoughts true or is there evidence against them?

◉   Are my standards too high? Am I just trying to be perfect?

◉   Was the situation really a complete disaster? Am I over-reacting?

◉   Was the situation really my fault or am I blaming myself for someone else's behaviour?

◉   How much do I want this situation to affect my life? Is it really that important?

◉   How would someone else view this? What advice would I give someone else in my position?

There are a number of reasons why therapy is an important part of recovery. It can help you to discover the thoughts and beliefs that led you to develop the eating disorder. It can improve your levels of self-esteem and self worth. It can also help you to learn to limit your obsession with body shape and size, as well as dealing with your fears about eating and gaining weight.

Dieticians or nutritionists can give specific help with your diet and arrange a healthy eating plan. They can support and encourage both sufferers who need to gain weight and those who need to lose. You may be asked to keep a food diary so that your dietician can check on your progress.

Alternatively, you might be referred to group therapy, which is available to sufferers on an in-patient, day patient or out-patient basis. Studies have shown that the most helpful group therapies are those that focus on problem-solving tasks, teaching skills or dealing with conflict issues. Since many eating disorder sufferers isolate themselves, a group situation may feel threatening but it can also be very beneficial. Hospitals and eating disorder units often run many different courses such as assertiveness training, body image workshops and anxiety management classes.

Another way to get in touch with your feelings is through role-play. This can be undertaken in one-to-one sessions with your therapist or in a group situation (always with a therapist present). Together with the therapist, you role-play a situation that made you angry or upset in the past. This time however, instead of swallowing your feelings, you are allowed to express them. If you were angry then you can now shout out loud. If you were upset then you can cry. This kind of therapy may be difficult though and there has to be an agreement that no one gets hurt, since you may find yourself becoming very angry.

There are many potential problems that you could encounter during therapy. However, it is important that you do not allow these to stop you from choosing recovery. If you start to attend therapy sessions and find that the therapist is moving too fast for you then talk to them. Remember that you are in control of your recovery and if you need to take it more slowly, discuss this with your therapist.

If you are finding it hard to learn a particular approach such as Cognitive Behaviour Therapy, again talk with your therapist. This is not an easy therapy to learn at first so ask them to go a little slower. It is important not to take your old behaviour patterns into treatment with you. Don't try to be the 'best' or to get your therapy perfect the first time that you attempt it.

It is crucial that the sufferer understands that recovery is frequently a long and often painful process. The doctor or hospital alone cannot 'cure' the patient. However, they can work as a team with the sufferer and together reach a full recovery. The sufferer needs to be very open and honest for the treatment to work though. Most of all, they need to be honest with themselves and not pretend that they are going for recovery while still keeping all their eating disorder habits. A therapist once said to me that even if I couldn't always be honest with my doctors, I should never lie to myself about what I was feeling.

Starting recovery

There are many practical steps towards recovery that you can take at home. It is important to remember that recovery will mean giving up your negative behaviours around food. It will also mean that you need to allow your weight to reach a healthy level for your body. Recovery is not an easy process and it does require lots of support and encouragement from those around you. The following are some tips that may help you as you start recovering:

- Set yourself realistic goals. Aim to reach small targets so that you feel encouraged and positive about your recovery. If you try to tackle too much then you are likely to fail, which will not help to build your self-esteem.

- Be gentle with yourself. If you do not always reach your targets, do not treat yourself harshly. You are going to find that there are times when you feel unable to make any progress. At these times, just try to stay stable and not take any steps backwards.

- Write yourself a list of all the things that you will be able to do when you are well. It can help to read through this list when you are having a bad day, as it can keep you motivated.

- Try to praise yourself for your achievements. You may have found it hard to praise yourself in the past and frequently focused on your failings instead. Now it is time to look at your progress rather than concentrating on any setbacks that you may have had.

- For anorexia sufferers, gaining weight is likely to feel very difficult. You may feel intensely guilty and want to disappear into your eating disorder again. The feelings of guilt will pass but only if you face them. As you reach a healthier weight, you will find that food and your body shape will not longer be the sole focus of your life. When you gain weight, you may also find yourself experiencing emotions that were previously hidden by the eating disorder. If you are struggling to cope with these feelings alone, ask your therapist or support network for more help.

- Try to start to take control of your life. You may have previously allowed your eating disorder to rule you life and make all your decisions for you. Now is the time to begin focusing on what you want from your life. Your social life may be very limited and so you may want to slowly start to change that. How about a trip to the cinema with a friend?

Obesity

Men who suffer from severe or morbid obesity will require medical intervention in the same way as sufferers who are underweight. It is important that they are given regular health checks and guidelines to follow. As with all major life changes, it is important to make slow, definite dietary alterations which will be permanent rather than temporary. A slow steady weight loss for those who are overweight (and equally a slow weight gain for those who are underweight) is advisable. In particular, 'yo-yo' weight gain and loss can have a very negative affect on the heart.

There are many types of treatment available for obesity. Exercise and sensible eating are, of course, very important. If the patient has been given clearance by a doctor, then regular low level activities such as walking or gardening can be started. They will gradually increase the amount of gentle exercise until it reaches between 3-5 hours per week. The goal is not merely to lose weight but to manage to maintain a healthy weight for the individual's body type.

As with other medical conditions, in certain circumstances prescription medications may be appropriate. However, weight-loss medications should only be used by patients who are at increased medical risk because of their obesity, and it is vital that they are prescribed and monitored by a doctor. The most common prescription medication for weight-loss are 'appetite-suppressants'. These promote weight-loss by decreasing the appetite or increasing the feeling of being 'full'. However, it is very important that increased physical activity and a healthy diet are also adopted in addition to the medication. Reliance on 'appetite-suppressants' is not a solution to the problem.

Occasionally, surgical procedures such as stomach stapling are recommended if the patient's life is at risk. These are very drastic solutions and should only ever be undertaken in an emergency when all other options have been exhausted.

Building muscle

There are a growing number of men who are dissatisfied with their weight but unlike women (who would nearly always like to lose a few pounds), around 50% of men would like to gain some extra muscle. There are healthy ways that young men and teenage boys can safely build their muscles but it is important that they take great care in doing this.

It is possible to increase weight and muscular build by taking in more calories than are used each day. Added to that, carefully controlled strength training and aerobics will help build lean muscle mass. It is very important not to train every day since this can actually damage muscles and hinder their development. Another key point to remember is that there are no 'quick fix' solutions. Anabolic steroids are seriously dangerous as a bulking-up agent and should be avoided. It is advisable to obtain professional advice whenever you are undertaking a fitness programme so that you have the appropriate support. You may also wish to join a gym or employ a personal trainer who will advise you about the safest methods of building your muscles.

Tools for recovery

You may have heard talk about the 'tools of recovery'. These 'tools' are the approaches that will help you through the process of recovery. One of the most commonly used recovery tools is writing a diary or journal. In this journal, you can write down all your thoughts and feelings. These will frequently be the difficult and painful feelings associated with your eating disorder but do not forget to also include the positive feelings you experience when you reach a target or goal. Always be honest in your journal and if you are, it can help to chart your recovery.

Often, therapists set their patients different topics to write about and this will be easier if you are already used to writing down your feelings. By setting you different topics to write about, the therapist allows you to explore your feelings. You are likely to find that you learn a lot about yourself, your family and why your eating disorder developed. These are some possible topics you may want to write about in your journal:

- Describe ten good events in your life and ten bad events.

- Write about some of the comments that have hurt you most in your life.

- Write down some of your dreams or nightmares.

- List five good qualities that you have.

- List ten of the 'rules' that you have drawn up for yourself since your eating disorder began.

It may be that the key to ending their battle with eating disorders is for sufferers to actually reconsider the 'ideal male body image'. It can help to realise that we are frequently manipulated by the media and will accept what they put forward as the 'ideal'. Stop and rethink why you are exercising or dieting. Is it for the sake of your health or is it actually to the detriment of your health?

Are you dieting and exercising purely to try and change your appearance? If this is the case then it is necessary to look at why your image is so important to you.

It could be that you believe that your self-esteem would improve if you felt you looked better. If this is the case, you need to discover why your self-esteem has been lowered in the first place.

For a full recovery to take place, there are a number of factors that need to be addressed. It is important that a sufferer understands exactly what recovery entails before they embark on the process:

- The sufferer will need to discover his true personality and develop a sense of self. He needs to be able to express all aspects of his personality openly, not just those his family finds acceptable. This means that he will need to allow himself to show anger and aggression, as well as other difficult emotions such as sadness.

- Sufferers have to learn how to control their lives without their eating disorder. Although it has felt as though they had control over their lives by using their eating disorder, it was actually the disorder that controlled them. They will need to learn to make decisions and take actions without turning to their eating disorder for 'help'.

- They also need to look at many of the issues that were hidden by their eating disorder. Problems such as dependence on their parents and a desire to remain a child need to be addressed. They will have to learn to separate themselves emotionally from their closest relatives.

- Finally, they have to come to terms with their own feelings about their body and discover why the eating disorder developed in the first place. Often, group therapy can help men to talk openly about their feelings in a safe environment. They can see that other male sufferers share their feelings and this helps them to feel less alone.

Practical steps towards recovery

When you are suffering from an eating disorder, you need to deal with both the physical and mental problems associated with the illness. You have to change both the way you think and the way you behave. The following are some practical steps you can take towards stopping certain negative behaviours.

How to stop bingeing

Whether you suffer from anorexia, bulimia, bulimarexia or compulsive over-eating, it is likely that you have at some time struggled with bingeing. Feelings of hunger often lead a sufferer to start bingeing. They then feel guilt that they have eaten and will try to fast for as long as possible. This leads to hunger developing again and the cycle is repeated. To prevent binges starting, sufferers need to do the following:

- Eat regular meals so that your blood sugar does not drop too low (which can trigger cravings).

- If you do have a binge, do not skip a meal as this can lead you back into the cycle of disordered eating.

- If you do binge, do not vomit afterwards as this is very dangerous for your health.

- Try not to ever miss a meal. If you know that you will be out at a meal-time, take a snack with you to prevent yourself from getting too hungry.

- Try to avoid alcohol and/or drugs since these can affect your appetite.

- Your journal can again help you to stop bingeing. Start by writing down whenever you binge and your feelings at that time. Bingeing is not just a physical response to hunger. Many sufferers turn to food when they are feeling depressed, lonely or angry. Write down how you felt before your binge, during the binge and afterwards as well. Over time, you will begin to see a pattern forming and then you can start to set yourself some new rules.

- If you are bingeing several times each day, try to cut down and limit yourself to just one or two a day.

- Work out your 'danger times'. These are the occasions when you are most likely to binge. Try to make sure that during these times, you ask for extra help from family or friends.

- Write down the reasons why you binge and start to look for solutions to these problems.

- Try to distract yourself from bingeing. Talk to friends, write in your journal or start an activity that keeps your mind occupied.

- When you feel the need to binge, do not allow yourself to go food shopping.

If you do have a binge, do not be hard on yourself. Everyone has setbacks during their recovery. Work out exactly why you had the binge and see if you can avoid this problem in the future.

How to stop vomiting

This section will mostly apply to bulimics, although some anorexics do vomit at times during their illness.

If you only vomit occasionally, try turning to your journal to help you beat this part of your illness. Write down every time that you vomit and the reason why you felt you needed to do this. After about a month, you should be able to see a pattern in your behaviour. If you have vomited four times in a month, set yourself the task of only vomiting three times the next month. Gradually cut down your vomiting a small amount at a time until you are able to stop the behaviour altogether.

If you are vomiting numerous times every day then your diet is likely to have gone completely out of control. You may be using vomiting as a way to deal with any worries and anxieties you may have. Start by writing down your feelings before, during and after you vomit. If you are going to stop vomiting, you will need to discover a new way to deal with your feelings. The UK NICE guidelines (January 2004) have now confirmed that Cognitive Therapy is a practical way to deal with the behavioural problems associated with bulimia.

If you are going to control your vomiting, you need to look at how long you leave between eating and vomiting. If this is five minutes then you need to set yourself the task of waiting for ten minutes before you allow yourself to vomit. Do this for a week until you feel comfortable with this gap of time and then set yourself the task of waiting 20 minutes before you vomit. As you gradually become comfortable with this, lengthen the time period again. Remember to set yourself realistic targets that you can reach and do not rush your recovery.

You are likely to feel anxious during these 'waiting' time periods and so try to distract yourself with Cognitive Therapy or relaxation exercises. Ring a friend, talk with family members or take up a new hobby that keeps you occupied. Don't forget to reward yourself when you reach a target. You may have stopped buying presents for yourself when your eating disorder developed and now is the time to start again.

How to stop taking laxatives and diuretics

If you have been taking laxatives or diuretics for a long time then you are likely to experience some side effects if you suddenly stop taking them. Your body may swell slightly as you retain water (also known as oedema). To avoid this problem, you will need to cut down slowly on the number of pills you are taking. If you experience any problems such as oedema when you stop taking laxatives, it is important that you consult your family doctor.

You may also find that you become constipated when you cut down on the number of laxatives that you are taking. This can leave you feeling bloated and uncomfortable because you are used to feeling very empty after taking laxatives. You need to accept that the 'empty' feeling is an unhealthy one, brought on by an overdose of medication and that feeling full is a natural part of life. You will also need to alter your diet to prevent serious constipation.

As you cut down on laxatives, you will need to eat more fibre. It is important to start slowly with cooked fruit and vegetables. A hot drink in the morning can help your bowels to start working properly. Do not eat large amounts of wheat bran though since this causes wind, stomach bloating and lowers the calcium levels in your body. Oat bran is a healthier alternative to wheat bran.

In addition, every time you cut down on one laxative, add an extra dried prune or dried apricot to your diet. As you cut down on the number of laxatives you are taking, also increase the amount of water you are drinking. You need to drink at least six glasses of water each day. When you have completely cut out all laxatives, start adding raw fruit and vegetables to your diet.

It is important to let your doctor know that you are trying to cut down on laxatives. If you are experiencing serious constipation, they will be able to prescribe a mild medication to help you through this difficult time. Although it may take a few months to adjust, your bowels will adapt to functioning healthily again without laxatives.

How to stop over-exercising

If you are suffering from anorexia, bulimia or muscle dysmorphia, it is likely that you are at times over-exercising. Exercising may be a way for you to block out difficult thoughts and feelings, and again you will need to learn to cope with these in a healthier manner. Exercise should be something that you enjoy in small amounts in order to remain healthy. You should not feel physically exhausted at the end of a session. It is recommended that adults exercise for about thirty minutes, four to five times each week. Once people exercise above this level then the health benefits decrease and there is a higher risk of injury.

Again, use your journal to record exactly how much physical exercise you are doing each week. Write down your feelings, before, during and after the exercise period. If you are exercising for an hour every day, start by cutting down to 50 minutes each day. Make sure that you cut down slowly on the amount of exercise you are doing and gradually replace it with more sedentary activities.

It is vital that your weight is at a healthy level if you are to follow a healthy exercise plan. As anorexia sufferers increase their weight to a healthy level, it is advised that they start gently exercising to begin toning wasted muscles. However, it is important that medical professionals supervise this kind of exercise programme.

How to stop weighing and measuring yourself

Most eating disorder sufferers weigh themselves frequently each day, often before and after meals. In a similar way, sufferers of muscle dysmorphia will measure their body numerous times every day. Both of these behaviours are unhealthy and it is important to learn how to stop them.

Frequent weighing sessions will also give inaccurate results. Everyone's weight varies between one and four pounds each day and to gain an accurate reading, it is important to only weigh yourself once a week. Make sure you do this at the same time every week and that you are wearing the same clothes. Once you have decided on the time and day each week that you will weigh yourself, you need to be very strict. This is the only time that you must allow yourself to stand on the scales.

If you feel it is impossible for you to cut down to just once a week then gradually reduce the number of times you weigh yourself daily. If you weigh yourself ten times a day, then limit yourself to only eight times for the next week. Gradually cut down on the number of times until you are just weighing yourself once a week.

If you are also measuring yourself frequently, cut down on the number of times that you are doing this by using the same method just described.

Learning how to relax

When you are trying to recover from an eating disorder, you are likely to experience periods of anxiety. Many therapists teach their patients relaxation techniques to help them deal with feelings of panic, especially before and during meal-times. Relaxation exercises do not work for everyone but they can help to lower levels of stress. When you first try to do them, you may find it difficult but do not give up too soon. The following are some common relaxation techniques:

Relaxation breathing

It is important to learn how to breathe properly during the relaxation exercises. Deep breathing alone can start to calm and relax you when you are feeling panicked. These are some of the principals of relaxation breathing:

- Start by breathing out so that you clear your lungs ready for the first deep breath.

- Breathe in through your nose and out through a slightly opened mouth.

- Breathe into your abdomen. Put you hand on your stomach and feel it rise as you breathe in and fall when you breathe out.

- Make sure that you breathe slowly or else you will hyperventilate.

- Focus on your breathing throughout the exercise. This becomes a form of self-hypnosis.

If you are having trouble with the breathing exercise, it can help to place one hand on your stomach and one on your chest. Concentrate on your stomach moving and your chest staying still. You will need to practice this exercise since it is difficult at first. Start by trying it for five minutes and gradually lengthen that time up to fifteen or twenty minutes.

Imagery

Another common relaxation exercise is the use of imagery. Start the exercise by taking three deep breaths to relax yourself. Then imagine that you are somewhere peaceful. People often visualise that they are on an empty beach, lying on the hot sand. Imagine that you can smell the ocean and hear the sound of the waves lapping at the shore. Feel your body relax in the warmth of the sun. Your imagery can be set in any location you like - a snowy mountain or in a boat on a lake for example. Wherever you choose, remember to use all your senses in the exercise and focus on touch, sight, smell, taste and sound.

Muscle relaxation

In 1929, Edmund Jacobson described a technique called Progressive Muscle Relaxation. This method of deep muscle relaxation reversed the muscle tension of a stress reaction. It involves focusing on each individual muscle group and letting them relax. Start at your toes and gradually work your way up the body. Focus on your toes, tense them and then relax. Repeat this and then move onto another muscle. Move through your body from feet to ankles, shins, calves, knees etc. As you let go of the tension in each muscle group, you will gradually feel your body relax from your feet upwards.

There are other way of relaxing that you may want to try when you are feeling panicked or tense. A hot bath can be very relaxing, especially if you also listen to soothing music. Gentle stretching exercises can loosen tense muscles, as can a short gentle walk. Try to discover which methods work best for you and use these to help you with your recovery.

Guided visualisation

Another form of therapy that can be very helpful for eating disorder sufferers is Guided Visualisation. This is a form of therapy which combines deep muscle relaxation with the suggestion of visual images. It has been found that repressed feelings and emotions are often brought to the surface during this process. As eating disorder sufferers tend to focus on their outer body, this therapy can help them to look inside themselves.

The following are two examples of guided imagery that can specifically help eating disorder sufferers:

⊙ This example relates to body shape and this can uncover many deep-seated issues.

Patients are told about three specific body types. These are V-shaped (the traditional 'ideal' male body shape), thin and overweight. They are then asked to imagine that they awake one morning in their 'perfect' body shape. They have to imagine proceeding through their day as this 'perfect' person. How would they dress, eat and interact with others, and how would other people respond to them? They are asked how they feel emotionally and what their body is saying to the world. Do they feel in control, powerful, happy, excited, masculine or feminine? Are they acting differently because they have a different body shape?

The exercise is then repeated with the other two body shapes that were first described to them. Again, they are asked to describe exactly how this body shape makes them feel. Finally, they are asked to describe the shape they aspire to and what statement this makes about them. All the comments that the patient makes during the exercise are then discussed in follow-up therapy sessions.

⊙ The following example of guided imagery is used to establish what the sufferer feels is the meaning of 'fat'.

'Fat' means different things to both men and women. When you mention 'fat' to women, they are likely to focus on the development of their breasts, stomach, thighs and hips. Men frequently see 'fat' as a sign of weakness and a lack of athleticism and strength. If a young man has had a close association with his mother during childhood, it is possible that he can feel he has developed a similarly rounded figure. Strict dieting to the point of extreme fasting can begin in an attempt to rid himself of any trace of fat and possible femininity.

During the visual imagery, sufferers are asked to imagine that they can 'laser' off all the fat from their body and watch it drip into a puddle on the floor. They are then asked how they feel when they look at the puddle of fat. Do they feel relieved that it is no longer part of their body? Or do they feel a sense of loss, as if something is missing from their life?

The next stage is for the sufferer to imagine that the puddle is coming to life and forming into a specific shape. They are asked what they feel it becomes, what it says or does and whether or not it is likeable. The sufferer then has to get to know this 'creature'. Is it part of themselves? Is it a part that they have disowned? Does it represent a specific person? Could it be their mother or father, a grandparent, friend or sibling? Is it a burden to them? Do they feel they need separation from it and why?

Finally, the fat melts back into the puddle and the sufferer has to make a choice. They need to decide whether they will leave it behind, accept it back into their body as part of themselves or carry it separately with them in a large sack. They are then asked to say exactly how they feel about their final choice and the pros and cons of it.

After the imagery has finished, the sufferer is asked to draw what the fat became during the visualisation and discuss exactly how it acted and what it meant to them. All of the information obtained during the exercise can again be discussed during follow-up therapy sessions.

Inductive reasoning

Inductive reasoning is a process that we all use throughout our lives. However, for eating disorder sufferers it can be a serious problem since it may result in keeping them trapped in their illness.

Inductive reasoning uses experiences and observations to form conclusions. We use our own knowledge and experience to make observations which we believe will always be true. In the case of an eating disorder sufferer, they will decide that since they currently feel fear at the thought of eating a meal, this fear will never disappear. They are using their previous experience to determine what will happen in the future.

As they have not had any experience of recovering from an eating disorder, sufferers therefore believe that it is not possible and so is not worth attempting. It is important for therapists to work with sufferers to show how recovery can be possible and to emphasis the value of small steps forward.

Many sufferers are also told that they are seriously damaging their health with their disordered eating. However, since they have not as yet experienced any physical side-effects of their illness, they are likely to dismiss their doctor's comments. This is another example of inductive reasoning at work. If they have not seen any health dangers appear yet, they can assume that this will never happen to them. It is vital to explain to sufferers both the short and long term negative effects of eating disorders on their physical and mental health.

Expressing emotions

One of the main problems that men experience is an inability to express their true feelings and emotions. They often see this as being a 'feminine' trait and not something that strong men should do. However, it is clear that pent-up emotions cause extreme problems and there are many different solutions to this.

Anger is a common emotion but expressing it correctly to the right person is very difficult. As the philosopher Aristotle said:

> "Anyone can become angry - that is easy - but to be angry with the right person, and to the right degree, and at the right time, and for the right purpose, and in the right way - that is not within everybody's power, that is not easy."

Men will often feel full of an unexpressed rage, which can lead them into problematic situations. Helpful ways to safely express these feelings include a controlled work-out (which is not excessive), punching or kicking a punchbag, playing video games and tearing up cardboard boxes or newspapers.

It is important to remember that anger is often the result of feeling afraid. If you find yourself frequently suffering from strong bouts of anger, it is advisable to look into the reasons for this.

Some final tips to help with recovery

If you are having trouble shopping, allow someone else to buy food for you. This can help all eating disorder sufferers. If you are anorexic then you are unlikely to be able to choose higher calorie foods for yourself and it can help to allow someone else to make the decision. If you feel that you overeat then asking someone else to shop for you will stop you purchasing foods that you find too tempting to resist.

Try not to keep comparing yourself to other people. Remember that we are all different and it is important to like yourself for who you are.

If you constantly look in mirrors at the size of your body, you might want to consider removing them from the house for a while. This can also apply to scales if you weigh yourself several times a day. These are not healthy behaviours and it can help to remove the temptation for a short period.

If you are anorexic and cannot accept how thin you have become, try this exercise. Lie down on the floor on a large piece of paper and allow someone (of a healthy body weight) to draw around your shape. Then you should ask them to lie on the floor while you draw around their shape. When you compare the paper afterwards it can help to clarify your actual size.

You may often read books or magazines about weight, food or fitness. If this is the case then try to stop it for a while. Constantly focusing on your body is not healthy. Use the money you save to treat yourself to a magazine that is not based around your obsession.

Have six small meals a day instead of three large ones. This can help all eating disorder sufferers. If you are anorexic, it can feel less intimidating to tackle small meals. If you are overweight, eating small meals regularly will increase your metabolic rate. You are also less likely to resort to bingeing since your blood sugar level will be constant.

Finally, remember to take your recovery slowly and reward yourself for all the progress that you make.

Chapter 12

Healthy Living

Today, the medical profession puts a lot of energy into promoting the idea of prevention rather than cure. Most of us have seen television adverts advocating high fibre diets for a healthy heart, as well as the regular anti-smoking campaigns. Some physical problems are unavoidable but many of the lifestyle-induced illnesses can be prevented.

However, it is not easy to make conscious, healthy choices when we are faced with so much temptation on a daily basis. Cheap convenience foods are readily available on demand in most shops and these can become a comfort when faced with the stresses of modern life.

The media sends out conflicting messages about food. We are bombarded with cookery programmes that teach us how to make rich desserts and high calorie meals, as well as adverts promoting fast food outlets and high calorie convenience snacks. However, we are also constantly exposed to the idea that being overweight is bad and that dieting is good. Men's magazines are quickly catching up with women's in advertising diet plans and products.

Nobody needs to go to extremes though. To lead a healthy life, the majority of people need a moderate amount of exercise and a healthy eating plan. When any form of exercise or food plan is taken to extremes then there is a high risk of health problems developing.

Alcohol and cigarette manufacturers target men in particular. Peer pressure and this intense level of media influence can therefore lead men to feel that they are not masculine if they do not drink four bottles of beer every night or smoke a certain brand of cigarettes.

A moderate amount of alcohol can be extremely beneficial to health. Research has repeatedly shown that men who drink between 1 and 10 glasses of red wine a week (though no more than 2 per day) appear to live longer. However, drinking too much is known to be detrimental to health. Alcohol can cause depression and, if taken to the extreme, becomes an addiction which can cause serious life threatening illnesses.

Positive self-esteem

Self-esteem determines how we feel about ourselves and how we react to other people. The ultimate goal is to obtain a healthy self-esteem without becoming arrogant or selfish. For example, research has shown that many rapists and other offenders often have very high levels of self-esteem, which allows them to think only of themselves and not consider other people's rights and needs. As a result, they are lacking in care and empathy for other human beings and will make themselves feel better by making others feel worse. Self-esteem cannot be built at the expense of other people.

Self-esteem also cannot be achieved purely through external factors. It has to come from within. Often men believe that a high-powered job and a good wage packet will build their level of self worth. To have good self-esteem though, you do not need 'perfect' looks, a 'perfect' body or the 'perfect' job. Alternatively, you will also not build up a good self-image if you constantly try to just please others.

From childhood, the way we react both to criticism and praise starts to form our levels of self-esteem. If a child is repeatedly told that they are not good enough at anything they do, they will gradually begin to believe that they are a failure. Children are exposed to a variety of influential people. If they experience judgmental teachers, resentful siblings, 'pushy' parents or bullies at school, this can seriously damage the child's development. Negative feelings about their own looks or body can, in time, lead to eating or exercise issues developing.

Damaged self-esteem is difficult to repair but not impossible. It does require a lot of hard work and frequently, external professional help. The first step is to try and stop yourself from always being self critical. We all make mistakes. Someone with good self-esteem accepts this and moves on. Someone who feels very negatively about themselves though will use even the smallest of errors as an excuse to beat themselves up.

The next time you make a mistake, try to be gentler on yourself. Think how you would treat a friend who had made a similar error. Would you yell at them and call them harsh and cruel names? Or would you try to comfort them and help them to start again?

People often use positive affirmations to help them retrain their negative thoughts. This can feel a little pointless or even silly at first but perseverance is very worthwhile.

Messages such as: 'I do deserve happiness', 'My weight does not need to control my life', 'I am allowed to have fun' and 'I am not a bad person' are a good starting point. For eating disorder sufferers, affirmations can prove to be a vital part of the recovery process.

How to build a positive self-image

When you have body image problems, it often feels unbelievable that you could ever feel good about yourself again. However, it is possible to alter your feelings if you start to gently make changes in your life. Below are some ideas of behavioural changes which can alter the way you feel about yourself in time:

⦿ **Understand that everyone is different.** Our body type is determined by our genetic makeup. If you are naturally a shorter and sturdier **endomorph** then however much you exercise or diet, you will never transform yourself into a tall and willowy ectomorph. It is important to see your body shape as part of your uniqueness. It would be a very boring world to live in if we were all identical.

⦿ **Start to look at advertisements and magazine images more objectively.** Is it really worth spending so much time trying to achieve that 'perfect' body? How many <u>real</u> people do you know who have the 'perfect' body? Male models have to spend all their time watching what they eat and exercising vigorously just to maintain their appearance. Sadly, many of them also suffer from eating or fitness related health problems. Do you really want that for yourself? Rather than constantly working hard to change your body, focus instead on accepting your body as it is. It is also important to remember that to retain a 'perfect' body takes many hours each day. Models find they spend most of their time working hard just to maintain their body. This will also become more difficult as time passes, since ageing is a natural fact of life.

⦿ **Accept that your masculinity or worth as a man is not linked to your shape or size.** Often, men feel that they are 'feminine' if they do not have a muscular body with a '**six-pack stomach**'. However, masculinity comes from within and it is not just about being strong and fearless. It is also about being sensitive, caring, co-operative and creative. These qualities, which are often mistakenly thought of as 'feminine', are vital masculine traits.

⦿ **Look for other qualities within yourself that you like and which are not focused on your appearance.** Try to develop these qualities rather than always striving to change your shape. For example, many people are artistic or creative but may not have sketched or drawn a picture since they were at school. Now is the time to start to discover yourself and find out your true capabilities.

⦿ **Learn some affirmations.** Constantly telling yourself that you are 'too fat', 'too thin', 'underdeveloped', 'ugly' or 'scrawny' is not going to build your self-esteem. Instead, you need to develop a positive self-talk that you use to counteract the negative messages in your head. Why do you need to be so cruel to yourself? Try to be a little kinder.

- **Are all your friends connected with your obsession?** Do you talk with people at the gym but not at work? Maybe it would be better to spend time with friends who are not obsessed with their weight or appearance. Being around people who eat healthily and normally can be very beneficial for eating disorder sufferers.

- **Look at the attitudes of people who feel comfortable in their own bodies.** They may not have the 'perfect' body but they are not obsessed with constantly changing themselves. Remember that being an individual is important.

- **Learn to be more assertive.** Teasing may be meant harmlessly but it is sometimes essential to explain how hurtful it can be. Try to have the courage to tell people when they have upset you.

- **Learn more about your body and the damage that occurs if you over-exercise or diet too rigidly.** Remember that you need to look after your body if it is going to serve you well throughout your life. It is important not to ignore how damaging severe dieting and over-exercising can be. What is the good of having a 'perfect' shape if your bones and joints are suffering because of your behaviour?

Allowing yourself pleasure

Many of us grow up believing that the most important part of our life is work. However, it is frequently said that at the end of their lives, few people wish they had spent more time in the office.

Pleasure is a vital part of our daily life but when self-esteem drops, a person usually believes that they no longer deserve the good things others take for granted. Eating disorder sufferers often deny themselves food as a way of punishing themselves for not being 'good enough'. They may even take it further and begin to self-harm in an attempt to punish themselves even more.

Part of recovering from an eating disorder is learning to allow yourself the simple pleasures of life. Often, sufferers will push away the people closest to them, even though what they desire most is the comfort of a reassuring hug. Start to reintroduce these small pleasures back into your life. This is frequently known as Exposure Therapy and requires the sufferer to take small steps outside of their rigid safety zone.

For your first task, do not choose something that feels totally impossible (such as buying an expensive item like a television for yourself) since this will feel too intimidating. Instead, buy a book, magazine or even just a cup of coffee that you would not normally allow yourself. Gradually, you can progress to larger pleasures but take it at your own pace and always ask for help and support if you feel yourself struggling and wanting to take steps backwards. Although it may feel very difficult at first, in time it will get easier until it eventually becomes a normal part of your daily life.

How to make changes

Whenever you choose to change anything in your life, it is always wise to follow certain basic rules:

- You need to actually decide to make the change. Often, people will point out certain aspects of your life that may need addressing. Ultimately though, you have to make the decision to change them.

- Learn as much as you can about the part of your life that you want to change. For example, if it is your diet then find out about the different kinds of fats, proteins, carbohydrates and fruit and vegetables your body needs, and what vitamins and minerals are required.

- Understand that change takes time. You are unlikely to see positive results immediately and patience is required so that you don't give up. If you persevere though, you will soon see many very positive results.

- Changes should be made slowly. If you try to change too much too quickly, it can lead you to feel afraid and wish to revert back to your original negative behaviour patterns.

- Set yourself realistic goals that are achievable and do not condemn yourself if you don't always hit your target the first time. Remember that you are trying to be kinder to yourself so don't think in terms of 'being a failure' if you do not achieve a goal.

- Keep in sight your reasons for making changes. Often, it is a difficult process and you will want to give up at times. It can help to write a list of the reasons why you have chosen to make these changes in your life.

- It is important to be aware that not everyone may be as happy as you are with the changes and the progress that you have made (either because they do not feel it is enough or because they actually preferred you to remain ill). Do not let their attitudes affect you though and remember why you are making these changes and their importance to your health and wellbeing.

- For eating disorder sufferers in particular, the reaction of those around them can sometimes lead them to misinterpret positive feedback. Many sufferers struggle when they are told that they are starting to look 'healthier'. They misinterpret the words 'healthy' and instead hear them as 'fat'. Remember that people were very concerned when you were dangerously thin and are now simply feeling relieved that you are looking healthier.

- Make sure that you reward yourself whenever you achieve one of your goals. Remember how difficult these changes have sometimes been to maintain and how much courage you have shown in persevering.

Chapter 13

Healthy Eating

If you are going to maintain a healthy weight then you need to adopt a healthy eating plan which does not involve restricting calories. It needs to be satisfying, pleasant and varied. To maintain physical health, it also needs to be combined with regular physical exercise and effective stress management. I do not like using the term "diet" however because that implies a restrictive short term programme, whereas healthy eating is for life and should not leave you feeling deprived in any way.

Why diets can be a negative experience

Diets are uncomfortable, both physically and psychologically. They are often expensive and involve the purchase of unusual products that you would not normally buy. Certain diets will encourage you to have milkshakes for breakfast and lunch, and then a cooked meal in the evening. This does not encourage you to build a lifelong healthy approach to food.

Diets are potentially dangerous, especially if they encourage the dieter to remove certain foods from their daily intake, such as proteins or carbohydrates. 'Fad' diets can even potentially be fatal, for example the 'water only' fasting diet from the 1980s, which resulted in several deaths. Dieters are often irritable and can experience negative mood swings. They are frequently preoccupied with thoughts of food and eating because the body is reacting to deprivation.

Often diets are unnecessary since the dieter is trying to reach an unrealistic weight level for their body. It is important to accept your natural healthy body size rather than trying to fight against it all the time. Diets are often quick-fix solutions that very rarely work in the long term, whereas a well-balanced healthy eating plan will be a permanent change for the better.

Male body shape

It is important to accept that we are all born with a specific body type. Ectomorphs are tall and lean, Mesomorphs are generally athletic and more muscular, whilst Endormorphs are of a larger build and broader. If you are an Endomorph, even the strictest of diets cannot change you into an Ectomorph.

It is very important to accept yourself for who you are and work with the material you have been given. No body type is inherently better or worse and each has its own merits and drawbacks. For example, ectomorphs find it hard to build muscle but they are often extremely good at endurance sports, such as long distance running.

Men who want to gain weight

There are about as many men who want to gain weight as want to lose it. This differs greatly from women, where the emphasis is almost exclusively on weight loss. Men who want to gain weight are usually interested specifically in building lean muscle mass. Again, the speed and ease with which a man gains weight and builds muscle is very dependent on his body type.

If a man is to gain weight beyond his natural point, he will need a combination of high calorie intake and strength training. This combination of intense muscle activity (gym based work) and adequate calories to support the desired growth will lead to increased muscle. However, the body does reach a natural maximum for its type and this inbuilt limit will prevent most men from gaining a 'classic' bodybuilder's physique.

Building muscle mass in a healthy way should be done through exercise and healthy eating rather than through 'bulk-up' programmes. As with dietary aids, there are many products on the market geared towards instant muscle growth. These usually promise very fast results for relatively little effort and buyers should exercise caution.

If you want to add muscle, try to set yourself realistic goals and do not expect immediate results. Also remember that muscles grow primarily when they are not being worked, so it is very important to give yourself days off inbetween your weight training regime.

A balanced diet

It is very important to remember that there is room in every healthy eating plan for treats. No food should be considered off limits completely and if you follow the general guidelines about healthy eating for the majority of the time, there is absolutely no harm in having occasional fast food meals, etc. Problems only occur when these meals become a regular part of each day and important nutritional staples such as fruit and vegetables are avoided.

Some food facts

⦿ Your daily intake should ideally be based around the following percentages: Carbohydrates (40%), fats (between 20-30%) and protein (30-40%).

- Try to eat monosaturated fats (found in olive oil) and avoid saturated fats (found in marbled meat and butter) and hydrogenated fats (found in margarine, coconut oil and palm oil) as much as possible. Polyunsaturated fats (found in corn and sunflower oils) are fairly neutral. This is because monosaturated fats are considered to be the most beneficial for the heart. Saturated and hydrogenated fats contain high levels of cholesterol, which can result in a dangerous build-up of plaque in the arteries.

- 40% of your daily intake should be complex carbohydrates. These include pasta, whole grains, bread and rice, etc. These foods release energy slowly throughout the day, which prevents sudden drops in blood sugar levels. This also prevents food 'cravings', which occur when you eat high sugar foods frequently. Although you get an instant rush of energy, this soon passes and you are left with a craving for more sugary food.

- Salt is an important part of a healthy diet but if it is used excessively, it can cause high blood pressure and heart problems.

- It is very important to keep the body hydrated and between 6-8 glasses of water should be drunk every day.

- Fruit and vegetables are a very important part of a healthy diet and ideally, around 5 servings should be eaten daily. For example, one serving could be an apple, half a grapefruit or a glass of fruit juice.

- 2-3 servings of protein should also be eaten daily. Protein is found in dairy foods (such as milk, cheese and yoghurt), meat, fish, eggs and vegetarian products (such as Quorn or tofu). Protein is also found in beans and lentils but the value is not quite so concentrated and a larger quantity needs to be eaten. One serving of protein is 2 eggs, 3-4 tablespoons of peanut butter or a glass of milk.

- 6-11 daily servings of carbohydrates are also essential each day. One serving is a slice of bread, an ounce of cereal or a cup of cooked rice or pasta.

- Foods that are higher in fat and sugar such as chocolate, butter, cakes, biscuits and mayonnaise can still be part of a healthy eating plan but they need to be eaten in moderation.

An average man needs to eat approximately 2500 calories per day. Some people may need to eat slightly more or less, depending on their size, metabolism and level of physical activity. I don't think it's wise for anyone to specifically count calories every day (because this can encourage obsessive thinking) so try to aim for a rough estimate using the diet plan I have set out here as a guide:

Sample Diet Plan (Containing approximately 2,200 calories)

Breakfast

> 40g muesli or 2 Shredded Wheat / Weetabix
>
> 1/3 pint of milk (semi-skimmed)
>
> 2 slices of toast (wholemeal)
>
> 2 teaspoons of butter
>
> 2 teaspoons of jam
>
> Tea / coffee with milk (semi-skimmed)

or

> 1 glass of fruit juice (250ml)
>
> 2 eggs scrambled with milk (semi-skimmed)
>
> 2 slices of toast
>
> 2 teaspoons of butter
>
> Tea / coffee with milk (semi-skimmed)

Total - 560 calories

11.00

> Tea / coffee with milk (semi-skimmed) + 2 digestive biscuits, muesli bar or small chocolate bar

Total - 150 calories

Lunch

> Jacket potato (200g) filled with
>
> 100g tuna + 20g mayonnaise, or 60g of cheddar cheese
>
> 1 tablespoon of butter with side salad

or

> 1½ rounds of sandwiches made with
>
> 3 slices of wholemeal bread
>
> 3 teaspoons of butter
>
> 40g of cheese + 1 tomato, or 80g of ham or chicken, or 60g of luncheon meat
>
> One yoghurt or other dessert of 150 calories
>
> 1 piece of fruit – apple / pear / banana / orange

Total - 720 calories

Afternoon (3.00pm)

> Tea / coffee with milk (semi-skimmed) + a piece of fruit

Total - 70 calories

Dinner	100g of chicken
	200g of roast potatoes
	100g of sweetcorn
	100g of peas
	100g of apple pie + single cream

or

200g of mashed potatoes (mashed with margarine)
2 thick pork sausages or 4 Vegetarian sausages
200g of baked beans
Piece of fruit

or

Any ready meal of approximately 500 calories
Any dessert of approximately 200 calories

or

Vegetable Burger
125g of chips
100g of sweetcorn
100g of broccoli cauliflower
One fruit yoghurt

Total - 700 calories

FINAL TOTAL – 2,200

Please remember that this is a very basic guideline for men to maintain their weight. It is important that you learn how much food your body needs each day to maintain a healthy weight. This varies for everyone and it is only through trying different foods that you will discover what is right for you. Also, try to vary your diet as much as possible. Eating the same foods every day not only becomes boring but it can lead to deficiencies in your diet.

A few general tips to help you eat healthily for life

◉ When you are having a meal, stop eating when you feel full. This may sound obvious but many people (men in particular) have difficulty recognising their natural limits. Food can become a substitute for other aspects of your lives (such as meaningful relationships or job satisfaction) and you can substitute eating for your feelings. It is important to learn to recognise when your body is full, rather than ignoring its signals and continuing to eat purely for the sake of it.

- It doesn't actually matter when you eat. Often, people are encouraged to eat three meals a day with healthy snacks in between. Unfortunately, this isn't always practical and you need to plan alternative arrangements that are suitable for yourself and your lifestyle. Studies have shown that people naturally balance their calorific intake during the day and if they have had an enormous breakfast for example, they usually compensate with a smaller lunch.

- As with physical exercise, it is important to set yourself achievable goals when switching to a healthy eating plan. For example, if you have lived a life eating only cheeseburgers, it is not realistic to think that you can switch overnight to eating five servings of fruit and vegetables every day. It is much wiser to gradually phase in the alterations so that you don't put yourself off with any sudden dramatic changes. Be patient. New tastes and patterns of eating will take a while to settle in so try not to rule any food out until you have tried it for a while.

- You should be able to see visible changes to your health when you switch to a new healthier eating plan. Cholesterol levels should drop, as will blood pressure and you are likely to feel physically better - more alive and less sluggish.

- Take an interest in the buying and cooking of food so that you start to learn the nutritional value of the various different types of food. When you are eating, take time over your meal. It takes about 20 minutes for the receptors in the stomach to tell the brain what is being eaten. It also takes this length of time for the stomach to indicate that it feels full. If you rush your meals, you are likely to eat much more than you actually need.

- Try to eat as much 'real food' as possible rather than turning to diet products, which are often full of chemicals and do not actually help with weight loss in the long term.

Conclusion

I hope that this book has provided some positive ideas about how to move forward with your life. If you are suffering from an eating disorder and have started to think that you would like to try for recovery, it is possible you may be feeling quite overwhelmed. When I was trying to decide whether to attempt recovery, it helped me to make a list of all the pros and cons of my illness. I carefully wrote down all the good and bad points of my eating disorder. How it was affecting my life? What was I losing because of the illness? Did I gain anything by remaining ill?

When I finally had the list complete, I looked down at the few positives I had managed to write about my anorexia and started to realise that these were negative as well. I felt that my anorexia kept me 'safe' and 'protected' from the world but why did I want to be protected? Living a full life may feel frightening and risky at times but it can also be exciting and fun.

I strongly recommend that you look at how your eating disorder is affecting your life. If you could take two things into a new life, what would you take? Would you take your eating disorder with you? Even if you do not feel that you are ready to attempt recovery, it is important to be honest with yourself about how your eating disorder is damaging your day-to-day living.

If you are already taking steps towards recovery, remember to give yourself plenty of praise for your achievements. Also, try not to be too hard on yourself if you have some setbacks. These are a natural part of recovery. Trying to be perfect is likely to have been one of the reasons why your eating disorder developed in the first place, so do not be afraid of the odd mistake. Everyone makes mistakes - that is part of being a healthy human being. However, if you are having trouble taking further steps forward then do not be afraid to ask for more help. Reaching out for more support shows that you are taking real control of your life.

If you are reading this book because you want to help a loved one who you feel has a problem, there are a few simple steps you can take. Simply offering to be there for them and to listen if they want to talk is likely to be of great benefit. It is natural to feel angry and upset at times but try to be as patient as possible. Remember that the sufferer is controlled by their illness and they feel depressed and frightened by the situation themselves. It is very important to work with the sufferer against the illness as a united team.

It is also essential to allow the sufferer to take their recovery slowly. Trying to change too much too quickly can force them back to the 'safety' of their disorder. A slow recovery is much more likely to be a permanent one.

Finally, I want to end by wishing you lots of luck. From personal experience, I know what it is like to suffer from a chronic eating disorder and feel very grateful that I am now in full recovery. Beating an eating disorder is never easy but it is very worthwhile.

Please feel free to visit my recovery website at **www.annapaterson.com**

My Story

From the age of three, I was mentally and sometimes physically abused by my Grandmother. She treated me badly in many different ways, repeatedly telling me that I was worthless, unloveable, ugly and fat even though I was none of these. She constantly played cruel tricks on me (such as force feeding me and abandoning me in shops) and gradually my self-esteem was destroyed. Many horrific memories remain, including the time when I was seven years old and my Grandmother forced me to walk through the Chamber of Horrors in Madame Tussauds. She told me that I was a revolting person and belonged in this place with all the other disfigured and damaged faces.

I saw my Grandmother every day in an attempt to protect my Mother. My Mother suffered from migraines and I realised that these headaches became worse whenever my Grandmother treated her badly. Quickly I learned that I could stop my Grandmother from being cruel to my Mother if I took all the abuse instead. I was too frightened to ever tell my parents about my Grandmother's ill treatment because she said that she would kill my parents if I spoke out about it, so I stayed quiet.

My Grandmother often told me that I was a failure and said that I would never do well at school. This caused me to work even harder at my studies and I would always complete my homework the night it was set. Even though my Gran didn't live with us, she was often in the kitchen with my Mother when I returned from school and I became afraid of going home. I began to join in all the after-school activities available, including swimming, hockey, computer studies and gymnastics. I was wearing myself out though and by the age of 13, my body was no longer able to cope with all the abuse and hard work and it began to shut down.

I developed glandular fever and after many months of illness was admitted to the children's ward of our local hospital. My Grandmother visited me every day and continued to whisper cruel words to me. At the same time, she told the doctors and nurses that she believed my parents were abusing me. The doctors decided to stop my parents from visiting so frequently and instead encouraged my Gran to visit more often. I became very unhappy and stopped eating, so the doctors prescribed adult doses of anti-depressant drugs.

Almost immediately, these powerful drugs caused me to start hallucinating. The doctors thought I was telling them lies to avoid doing my homework and just increased the dosage of the pills. The hallucinations became more frequent and I couldn't look at a page or blank wall without horrific images appearing before my eyes. A few days later another problem developed and I found that I was losing the ability to read and write. When I looked at a page of writing, the words began to swim and move around so that sentences became meaningless.

It took my parents a number of days to convince the doctors that I was telling the truth about my condition and the pills were stopped but the damage had already been done. After I left hospital, I slowly taught myself to read again with the help of a piece of card that isolated just a few words at a time. Over the next two years I became used to reading and writing in this way and took all my 'O' level classes during this period. It wasn't until I began my 'A' level studies that I was able to read and write normally again.

By the time I was 17 we were having serious family problems. To help with her migraines, my Mother had been on tranquilizers since I was six years old. Now, 11 years later, she was taking a massive cocktail of them together with some very strong painkillers. She had disappeared into her own fantasy world and was writing strange poetry and letters to the singer John Denver. My Grandmother told me that my parents' marriage was in trouble and that they were going to get divorced. She said that this was all my fault.

It was then that I decided I had to disappear. I felt worthless and as if all I did was cause problems. I believed that I no longer deserved food and so stopped eating. I didn't feel this was enough punishment though and also began to seriously self-harm. Trapped in an impossible situation, I realised I was developing anorexia.

For the next four years my weight slowly dropped. I managed to keep my illness under control while my life was relatively calm but as soon as there was any extra stress, that dormant monster anorexia reared its head again. I left college at 19 because I was bullied by a 'friend' and instead started work in a solicitors' office. The first three months were fine but in time my boss began to treat me badly. My Gran's treatment had led me to believe that I deserved to be abused by anyone and he soon realised he could sexually harass and humiliate me. This behaviour continued for over two years.

By the age of 21 I was very ill. Two days after my twenty-first birthday, my parents told me that I was ruining their lives and making them both ill. The guilt I felt was tremendous but I simply couldn't eat, even for them. I felt totally controlled by an anorexic 'voice' in my head that sounded just like my Grandmother. It told me I was fat and ugly and had to starve myself. It yelled loudly every time I ate, repeatedly telling me I was a very bad person. I was now completely obsessed with food and did everything possible to avoid eating. Unable to force myself to eat, I grew extremely weak and had to give up my job as a legal secretary.

My parents took me to our family doctor who was horrified by my weight loss and immediately sent me to see a psychiatrist at our local hospital. She diagnosed anorexia nervosa and I felt as if my deepest darkest secret had been discovered. I felt ashamed and very alone. I had to agree to see a psychiatric nurse once a week but the shame I felt left me unable to share my true thoughts and feelings with her. Misled by my confusing answers to her questions, the nurse disagreed with the original diagnosis and started to treat me for the illness M.E. (chronic fatigue syndrome).

Relieved that the nurse no longer believed that I was suffering from anorexia, I fell even deeper into the illness becoming more withdrawn every day. Just after Christmas I felt so desperate and alone that I attempted suicide. Halfway through the attempt, I realised that my Mother would return home to find my dead body and I just couldn't hurt her in that way. I felt that I had already caused her enough pain by what I believed to be my 'selfish' behaviour. I put away the knife and bandaged my bleeding wrist.

Later that year, my Father retired from his job and we all moved to Cornwall to try and escape from my Grandmother. I managed to avoid doctors for three months but eventually we had to join the local health centre. The doctor I saw was horrified by my condition. During my physical examination, the nurse had discovered that I was trying to cheat the scales and they realised that my weight was now at a life-threatening level.

After just three months in my new home, I was confronted by two doctors who wanted to admit me to hospital. I tried to beg them to allow me to stay at home but my Mother said that she could no longer cope and I was admitted to my first psychiatric hospital. I was put on complete bed rest because my weight was so low that the doctors were scared that I could have a heart attack at any time. I should have been safe in the hospital but my Grandmother still managed to reach me there. She sent me letters telling me that my parents did not love me and asking why I didn't just let myself die? Instead of showing the doctors this evidence of her abuse, just as my Gran had instructed, I carefully tore up the letters and hid them at the bottom of my waste bin.

After a month, I had gained six pounds and managed to convince the doctors to discharge me. I began weekly therapy that increased to daily therapy as my weight slowly began to fall again. I had left hospital determined that the anorexia would never win again but after a few weeks at home, it had regained control and the 'voice' was louder than ever. I was once again lying and cheating so that I could lose weight. I hated myself every time I pretended I'd eaten or hidden some food but I felt I had to obey that 'voice'. My parents tried to force me to eat more but this just led me to become even more cunning and secretive.

One horrific day, two years after my release from hospital, I managed to totally block the drainage system in our Cornish home. I can still remember the complete terror I felt when I heard my Father's words: *"She's really done it this time! I don't want to call her my daughter any longer!"* My Mother was equally angry and said that she didn't believe my Father would ever forgive me. I vowed never to hide food or cheat the scales again but anorexia is a very powerful illness and that whispering 'voice' in my head soon took back control.

Three years after the first hospital admission, my weight had dropped to its lowest ever. I was seeing a psychiatric nurse every day and he was measuring out tiny portions of food for me to eat but my body could no longer process solid food. Even though I was eating, I was losing more weight every day. I tried to fool the doctors into believing I was heavier than I really was but eventually my tricks were discovered and I found myself back in hospital again. This time I was admitted to an eating disorders unit 200 miles from my home, where I was told that I was now just hours away from death.

Looking in the bathroom mirror for the first time since my illness had begun, I saw how I really looked. I was a walking skeleton, with my skin stretched tight over bones. My face had become a skull and when I smiled, it looked like I was wearing a horror mask. For that brief period of time I could understand why everyone was so worried.

The hospital saved my life and I stayed there for six months, working hard at therapy sessions each day. I wasn't completely honest with the doctors though, as the anorexic 'voice' in my head was still very powerful. I had learned so much therapy over the years that I was just repeating it back to them without feeling anything. My occupational therapist did realise what I was doing though and decided to play me the REM song "Everybody Hurts". As I heard the lyrics about holding on and never giving up, I broke down for the first time and started to talk very vaguely about my Grandmother's abuse. When I was discharged from the hospital a few months later, I was physically better but mentally and emotionally I was still very ill.

For the next five years, I lived at home with my parents. The confidence I had developed in hospital slowly began to disappear. I had been able to talk and joke with anyone in the hospital but once I was home, I started to hide in my anorexic shell again. Gradually my weight dropped once more, although I managed to maintain it at a level just high enough to keep me out of hospital. I started my own needlework business but this just gave me another safe reason to stay hidden at home. I led a very isolated life, seeing only my therapists. The few times I went out were with my parents and we lived a very controlled, timetabled existence. I was an adult woman, living the life of a child.

At the age of 29 I felt that my life would never change. I believed that I would always have anorexia and although it stopped me from doing so much, I could see no other options. The loneliness eventually became too much to bear and I joined a pen pal club. Through this group I met Simon, who I soon learned also suffered from low self-esteem. For the first time in my life, I felt able to tell someone about the abuse and my anorexia. This was the real start of my recovery because Simon was able to show me that I was not the terrible person my Grandmother had always told me I was. Slowly I began to realise that I did not need to punish myself by starvation and self-harming. I learned to trust Simon's view of my body rather than my own distorted anorexic view.

Simon was the first person to show me unconditional love and after a few months, we became engaged. With Simon's help, my recovery continued and I am now living a fulfilled happy and healthy life. Recovery is not easy or quick and the fact that Simon was willing to stand by me however long this took gave me the courage I needed to keep making progress.

I decided to share my experiences in the hope that I could help other sufferers beat their eating disorders. I wrote my autobiography *Anorexic* and soon found that many people began writing to me to share their own experiences. I began to realise just how huge a problem eating disorders really were and how little practical information and advice there was available. This is was why I wrote *Diet Of Despair*, a self-help book for sufferers and their families. I have since also written *Running On Empty*, a novel for young people about eating disorders and friendship. Through my books, I hope that I will be able to help sufferers and their friends and families to fight these killer diseases.

Glossary

Abuse - To mistreat a person either mentally, physically or sexually.

Aerobic Exercise - Increases oxygen production by raising the heart rate, for example jogging, swimming etc.

Amphetamines - A drug that is used as a stimulant and which, at first, causes a person to feel very wide awake.

Appetite suppressants - Medications that stop a person from feeling hungry.

Assertiveness - An ability to put forward your point of view and opinion.

Bigarexia - Where a sufferer believes that they are much smaller than they actually are. Sufferers generally tend to focus on the size of their muscles in particular.

Bingeing - When a person eats large quantities of food in a short space of time.

Body Dysmorphic Disorder - An illness where the sufferer believes that parts of their body are extremely ugly.

Body Mass Index (BMI) - A method for indicating the weight status of adults and measures weight in relation to height.

Bulimarexia - An illness that combines the symptoms of both anorexia and bulimia.

Calorie - A unit of energy obtained from food.

Cognitive Behavioural Therapy - A form of therapy that uses positive thoughts to reverse negative thoughts and feelings.

Comfort food - Food that people turn to for comfort when they are feeling low, such as chocolate pudding.

Constipation - This is when someone has trouble passing waste products (faeces).

Counsellor - A trained professional who deals with mental and emotional problems. They use a combination of empathy, unconditional positive support and congruence (emotional honesty).

CPN - An abbreviation for Community Psychiatric Nurse.

Dehydration - A lack of water in the tissues of the body, often caused by vomiting or laxative abuse.

Depression - A mental state of great sadness.

Diabetes - A disease where there is too much sugar in the blood due to a lack of insulin.

Dietician - An expert in diet and nutrition.

Distortion - A misrepresented and warped view.

Diuretics - Otherwise known as water pills, these medicines increase the production of urine.

Dysfunctional - Not working properly.

Ectomorph - People with an ectomorphic body tend to be underweight. This is the typical 'model' build. They often have trouble putting on any weight, however much they seem to eat.

ED - An abbreviation for 'Eating Disorder'.

ED-NOS - An abbreviation for 'Eating Disorder Not Otherwise Specified'.

Electrolytes - Otherwise known as 'salts', these are chemicals such as potassium, sodium, magnesium and chloride which are necessary to keep the heart rate constant.

Emetics - A medicine used to make people vomit.

Endomorph - An endormorphic body is quite sturdy and not too tall.

Endorphins - A chemical produced naturally in the brain during exercise, which brings about a feeling of well-being and happiness.

Exposure therapy - A type of therapy whereby a sufferer slowly confronts their fears in a controlled environment.

Fasting - When a person goes without food for a number of hours or days (otherwise known as 'starving').

Genetics - The study of which characteristics we inherit from our parents.

Gonadatropin - A hormone that controls testosterone production.

Gynaecomastia - Affects men and is a slight enlargement of the breasts during puberty.

In-patient - When a patient is admitted for a stay in hospital.

Insomnia - Sleeplessness and restlessness at night.

Insulin - A hormone produced by the pancreas that controls the amount of sugar in the blood.

Internalise - To turn your feelings inwards.

Lanugo - A fine covering of dark hair that grows on the body of an anorexic.

Laxative - A medicine which causes the bowels to empty more often.

Liposuction - A surgical procedure in which pockets of excess fat are drained away.

Menstruation - The discharge of blood once a month (otherwise known as a 'period') when an egg is unfertilized.

Mesomorph - People with a mesomorphic body type tend to keep their weight very level. They are usually quite tall and angular in shape. They are generally more muscular than endomorphs. They can gain or lose weight quickly but usually keep their weight stable. Even at a young age, mesomorphs generally look slightly older.

Metabolic rate - The speed at which the body burns up food.

Metabolism - The way that the body uses food to keep itself functioning.

Obesity - A condition where the sufferer is at least 20% above the recommended weight for their height.

Obsessive-compulsive - A condition in which the sufferer feels compelled to repeat rituals and live by strict rules in the belief that it will keep them 'safe'.

Oedema - A condition where fluid collects in the body tissue, especially around the ankles.

Osteoporosis - An illness caused by a loss of bone mass, which usually develops in middle age. Bones become brittle and are at risk of breaking.

Out-patient - When a patient has treatment on a daily or weekly basis at a hospital or clinic but does not stay overnight.

Passive-aggressive - Expressing anger through indirect means.

Pituitary - A gland in the brain which releases hormones and works with the hypothalamus.

Pounds - A measurement of weight, which can be written as 'lbs'.

Psychiatrist - A medically qualified doctor who specializes in the treatment of mental and emotional problems.

Psychologist - A person who, although not a medical doctor, is specifically trained in the treatment of mental and emotional problems.

Puberty - When a young person's body begins to change in preparation for adulthood.

Purging - When a person takes laxatives in large quantities to empty the body of all waste products.

Restrict - When a person is limiting their diet and avoiding certain foods.

Reverse anorexia - See 'Bigarexia'.

Rituals - A series of repeated behaviour patterns.

Section - When a doctor has to legally force a patient to accept treatment.

Self-esteem - Your own opinion of yourself.

Serotonin - An important substance for normal nerve and brain functioning. It is often associated with levels of happiness.

'Six-pack' stomach - Where a man's stomach is ridged so as to resemble a six-pack of beer.

Starvation - The condition caused when a person doesn't eat enough food.

Testosterone - A male hormone.

Vegetarian - A person who does not eat meat.

Vomiting - When someone is physically sick and brings up food they have recently eaten.

Weights

28 grammes = 1 oz

454 grammes = 1 lb

600 millilitres = 1 pint

16 oz = 1 lb

14 lbs = 1 stone

List Of Useful Addresses

Eating Disorder Associations (Worldwide)

Eating Disorders Association

First Floor, Wensum House
103 Prince of Wales Road
Norwich NR1 1DW
Telephone Helpline: 0845 634 1414 (8.30am - 8.30pm Weekdays)
Youth Helpline: 0845 634 7650 (4.00pm-6.30pm Weekdays)
E-mail: info@edauk.com
Website: www.edauk.com

National Association of Anorexia nervosa and Associated Disorders (ANAD)

P O Box 7
Highland Park
IL 60035
USA
Hotline: 847-831-3438
Fax: 847-433-4632
E-mail: info@anad.org
Website: www.anad.org

British Columbia Eating Disorders Association

526 Michigan Street
Victoria, BC
Canada V8V 1S2
Tel: 250.383.2755
Fax: 250.383.5518
Website: www.preventingdisorderedeating.org

Eating Disorders Association

P O Box 80 142
Green Bay
Auckland 7
New Zealand

Tel: 09 818 9561; 09 627 8493; 09 523 3531; 09 523 1308
E-mail: anorexia@health.net.nz
Website: www.everybody.co.nz/support/eating.html

The Eating Disorders Association

53 Railway Terrace
Milton
Queensland 4064
Australia
Tel: (07) 3876 2500

For after hours help - Lifeline: 131114

Children's Helpline: 1800 551800

Parents Helpline: 1300 301 300

Website: www.uq.net.au/eda/documents/start.html

Therapy and Counselling Organisations

The Institute of Family Therapy

24-32 Stephenson Way
London NW1 2HX
Tel: 020 7391 9150
Fax: 020 7391 9169
Website: http://www.ift.org.uk/

United Kingdom Council for Psychotherapy

167-169 Great Portland Street
London W1W 5PF
Tel: 020 7436 3002
Fax: 020 7436 3013
E-mail: ukcp@psychotherapy.org.uk
Website: www.psychotherapy.org.uk

United Kingdom Register of Counsellors

P O Box 1050
Rugby
CV21 5HZ
Tel: 0870 443 5232
Fax: 0870 443 5161
E-mail: bacp@bacp.co.uk
Website: www.bac.co.uk

Other Useful Organisations

Childline
Freepost 1111
London N1 0BR
Tel: 0800 1111 (Open 24 hours a day, 7 days a week)
Website: http://www.childline.org.uk/

The Samaritans
Tel: 0845 790 9090 or 0114 245 6789 (help 24 hours a day)
E-mail: jo@samaritans.org
Website: www.samaritans.org.uk

Victim Support (England and Wales)
Cranmer House
39 Brixton Road
London
SW9 6DZ

Supportline

Tel: 0845 30 30 900
(Low-call rate: 9.00 am - 9.00 pm weekdays, 9.00 am to 7.00 pm weekends)
Tel: 020 7735 9166
Fax: 020 7582 5712
E-mail: contact@victimsupport.org.uk
Website: www.victimsupport.org.uk